HIERARCHICAL
OBJECT-ORIENTED
DESIGN

PRENTICE HALL
OBJECT-ORIENTED
SERIES

B. MEYER
Eiffel: The Language

D. MANDRIOLI AND B. MEYER
Advances in Object-Oriented Software Engineering

B. MEYER
Eiffel: The Libraries

B. HENDERSON-SELLERS
A Book of Object-Oriented Knowledge

M. LORENZ
Object-Oriented Software Development: A Practical Guide

HIERARCHICAL OBJECT-ORIENTED DESIGN

PETER J. ROBINSON

PRENTICE HALL

NEW YORK   LONDON   TORONTO   SYDNEY   TOKYO   SINGAPORE

First published 1992 by
Prentice Hall International (UK) Ltd
Campus 400, Maylands Avenue
Hemel Hempstead
Hertfordshire, HP2 7EZ
A division of
Simon & Schuster International Group

Typeset in 10 on 12pt Times Roman by
Keyboard Services, Luton

Printed and bound in Great Britain by
Dotesios Ltd, Trowbridge, Wiltshire

Library of Congress Cataloguing-in-Publication Data

Robinson, Peter J. (Peter Jeremy)
    HOOD : hierarchical object-oriented design / Peter J. Robinson.
      p. cm.
    Includes bibliographical references and index.
    ISBN 0–13–390816–X (pbk.)
    1. Object-oriented programming (Computer science)   I. Title.
QA76.64.R63   1992
005.1'2–dc20   92-16817
                                              CIP

British Library Cataloguing in Publication Data

A catalogue record for this book is available from the British Library

ISBN 0–13–390816–X

---

1 2 3 4 5   96 95 94 93 92

CONTENTS

Editor's preface   ix
Preface   xi

1 INTRODUCTION   1

1.1 History and objectives   1
    1.1.1 ESA activities   1
    1.1.2 ESA software engineering life-cycle   3
    1.1.3 Ada design method development   5
    1.1.4 Shortlist of methods   6
1.2 Rationale for the HOOD approach   7

2 HOOD METHOD   11

2.1 Design process   11
2.2 The Basic Design Step   14
    2.2.1 Phase 1. Problem definition   15
    2.2.2 Phase 2. Development of the solution strategy 16
    2.2.3 Phase 3. Formalisation of the strategy 17
    2.2.4 Phase 4. Formalisation of the solution 18
2.3 Application of the Basic Design Step   19
    2.3.1 Root object   20
    2.3.2 Terminal object   21
2.4 HOOD Chapter Skeleton   22

3   FINDING OBJECTS AND OPERATIONS   25

3.1 Object definition   25
     3.1.1 Definition of an object   26
     3.1.2 Definition of a HOOD object   27
3.2 How to find objects: HOOD text approach   34
3.3 Operations   41
3.4 How to find objects: data flow diagram approach   43
3.5 Conclusion   50

4   HOOD DIAGRAMS   51

4.1 Passive and active objects   51
     4.1.1 Passive objects   51
     4.1.2 Active objects   52
4.2 Passive and active design   54
4.3 Operations   55
4.4 Include relationship   56
4.5 Implemented_By link   57
4.6 Use relationship   59
4.7 Uncle object   65
4.8 Operation_set   66
4.9 Data flow   67
4.10 Exception flow   69
4.11 Environment object   72

5   OBJECT DESCRIPTION SKELETON   75

5.1 Object Description Skeleton structure   75
5.2 Object definition   78
5.3 Provided interface   79
5.4 Required interface   82
5.5 Data and exception flows   84
5.6 Object Control Structure   85
5.7 Internals   87
5.8 Operation Control Structure   91
5.9 Pseudocode guidelines   94
5.10 HOOD pragmas   97

6   CLASS AND INSTANCE OBJECTS   100

6.1 Class object development   100
6.2 Class objects   101
6.3 Instance objects   104
6.4 Examples of class and instance objects   107
6.5 Static object inheritance   110

7 *REAL-TIME DESIGN* 112

7.1 Concurrency 114
7.2 Constrained operations 115
7.3 Object Control Structure 119
    7.3.1 OBCS definition 119
    7.3.2 FIFO queue example 123
    7.3.3 HOOD tasking pragmas 125
7.4 Op_Control object 126

8 *ADA SOURCE CODE GENERATION* 129

8.1 Ada code mapping 129
8.2 Visibility and scope 135
    8.2.1 Visibility inside and between objects 135
    8.2.2 Scope 136
8.3 Code implementation process 136
8.4 Designing types 138
    8.4.1 Defining types 138
    8.4.2 Types of types 139
    8.4.3 Mixed declarations of types and constants 141
    8.4.4 Task types 141

9 *DISTRIBUTED SOFTWARE DESIGN* 143

9.1 Virtual node object 143
9.2 Virtual node object diagram 144
9.3 Virtual node object ODS 146
9.4 Designing a program with virtual node objects 148

10 *DEVELOPMENTS OF HOOD* 155

10.1 CASE tools 155
10.2 HOOD in the software development life-cycle 159
    10.2.1 Interface to requirements 159
    10.2.2 System configuration 160
    10.2.3 Reuse of objects 160
    10.2.4 Global type package 161
    10.2.5 Abstract data type model 162
    10.2.6 Prototyping 163
    10.2.7 Testing 164
    10.2.8 Verification and validation of a HOOD design 164
    10.2.9 How to review a HOOD design 166
    10.2.10 Quality assurance 167
10.3 Future extensions to HOOD 169
    10.3.1 Object life-cycle 169
    10.3.2 Object-oriented language support 171
    10.3.3 Additional HOOD features 172
10.4 Standard Interchange Format 173

Appendices

A   HOOD method summary   175
B   HOOD Chapter Skeleton   177
C   HOOD reserved words   178
D   Heating system requirements   180
E   Sample design: traffic lights   181
F   ODS of class object **lights** and instance object **lights_ac**   204
G   ODS of active objects **FIFO_Queue** and **Interrupt**   210
H   ODS of Op_Control objects **start** and **push**   217
I   Ada language features   221
J   Glossary and abbreviations   227

Bibliography   233
Index   235

EDITOR'S PREFACE

The potential interest of object-oriented development for real-time and process-control applications has caught many people's attention. But there remains a certain reluctance to apply the object-oriented approach in large mission-critical applications. The contribution of HOOD here is essential, as few, if any, other methods in the field have stood the test of application to sizable real-time projects.

The HOOD method (the initials stand for hierarchical object-oriented design) was commissioned by the European Space Agency and developed by CISI Ingénierie. The original version was explicitly meant for software to be developed in Ada. Probably for that reason, it did not support the full range of object-oriented concepts, focusing instead on modularity, data abstraction, information hiding, hierarchically structured abstract machines, and of course support for concurrent execution and real-time applications. The importance of classes and inheritance was later recognised, however, and the method as described in Peter Robinson's book now supports these concepts. It may be used in conjunction with object-oriented languages, while retaining its compatibility with Ada.

Although there have been a number of articles on HOOD and a tutorial by Maurice Heitz at TOOLS conference, the method has not received so far the wide coverage that it deserves. The present book should help correct this situation. Peter Robinson has for a long time been involved in HOOD, and played a major part in its evolution. By acting as consultant to many projects using HOOD and training numerous people in the method, he has gained an in-depth mastery of the concepts and of their application.

Readers will benefit from this experience through the many examples and the case study of the Appendix. They will also gain precious insights about how the method should be applied in practice, learn about the possible pitfalls, and discover what it takes to apply the object-oriented approach, with all its potential benefits, to the tricky case of real-time systems.

PREFACE

This book is based on the definition of the syntax and semantics of hierarchical object-oriented design (HOOD) as presented in the *HOOD Reference Manual Issue 3.1.1*, published in February 1992, and on the HOOD method as presented in the *HOOD User Manual Issue 3.0*, which was published in December 1989 to complement the earlier *HOOD Reference Manual Issue 3.0*.

The changes introduced in *Issue 3.1.1* as developments from *Issue 3.0* are minor from a technical viewpoint, but the document has been changed more significantly, omitting, for example, a detailed section on Ada mapping. The *HOOD User Manual*, which defines the HOOD method, has not yet been updated to reflect these changes. This book may serve as a HOOD user manual until the HOOD Technical Group completes this work.

One of the reasons for writing this book is that many readers of *the HOOD Reference Manual Issue 3.0* did not see the *HOOD User Manual Issue 3.0*, and consequently had only a partial view of HOOD, which is not only a notation but, much more importantly, also a method. This has been a serious disadvantage to these readers, and has lead to criticisms about HOOD, some of which are due to having only partial information. The author hopes that this book will remedy this lack of information for the current version of HOOD.

Although HOOD was conceived with Ada as the programming language in mind, the *HOOD Reference Manual Issue 3.1.1* is written in more general terms, and HOOD is now starting to be used with C++ as the target language. Chapter 10 of this book outlines the variations needed when thinking in C++ terms. These comments also apply to other object-oriented languages.

The book includes several examples to illustrate the didactic parts of the text. There is also a complete sample design as an appendix. As examples, they are intended to be simple, so that they can be understood by readers from diverse backgrounds.

ACKNOWLEDGEMENTS

This book has evolved from the materials and experience of the HOOD method and HOOD toolset courses that I have developed and presented for SD-Scicon (UK) Training Limited, to whom I am grateful for permission to use this material. I have also previously published papers on HOOD in two books in the Unicom Applied Information Technology Series published by Chapman and Hall.

I would like to acknowledge the excellent contributions made by the original developers of HOOD in the first ESA contract, the other members of the HOOD Working Group in 1990 and the members of the HOOD Technical Group in 1991. These include Maurice Heitz of CISI Ingenierie, Jean-François Muller of Matra Espace, Klaus Grue of CRI A/S, and Joel Bacquet and Elena Grifoni of the European Space Agency. I would like also to thank Tony Elliott of IPSYS Software plc and Simon Handley of Birmingham Polytechnic for their many useful comments on the draft of this book.

HOOD is a trademark of the HOOD User Group (HUG). This fact must be stated in any publication referencing the name of HOOD in the context of the HOOD method as the basis of the publication. A revised version of the *HOOD Reference Manual* was published as *Issue 3.1.1* in February 1992, and is available from the HOOD User Group at the following address:

Finn Hass (HOOD User Group Chairman)
CRI A/S
Bregnerodvej 144
DK-3460 Birkerod
Denmark
Tel. +45(45)822100

The HOOD User Group may also be contacted through the author.

1

INTRODUCTION

1.1 HISTORY AND OBJECTIVES

Hierarchical object-oriented design (HOOD) is an Ada design method. That is to say, HOOD was specifically developed as an architectural design method for software to be written in Ada. The main reason for HOOD's success in being adopted for a wide range of Ada projects is probably that it was developed with the clear objective of supporting the architectural design phase of the software engineering life-cycle with a specific target programming language in mind. We look into the life-cycle as defined by the European Space Agency (ESA) shortly, but first let us look at the background in ESA prior to the development of HOOD.

1.1.1 ESA activities

I joined the European Space Agency in 1976 to work as a software engineer in the Spacelab project. ESA, like NASA, is an agency that acts as a customer on behalf of the governments that provide the funds, to procure space systems and to manage research and development programmes from companies in the aerospace industry throughout Europe, Canada and the United States. My role, therefore, was to act as a customer in the project which was procuring Spacelab from industry. In this case, the customer role was to supervise requirement definition, to review technical progress in the development of the software by attending reviews at each stage of the life-cycle, and finally to accept the software by participating in the full acceptance process. Given the complexity of an embedded system in which all the hardware and software was new, the requirements generally uncertain, and the contractors spread across Europe, this approach of continuous involvement was needed to ensure that quality was developed into the end-product. The final part, acceptance, was very important because although each of the companies involved had its own quality assurance staff, there are always divided loyalties between concern for the software quality and for the company's commercial needs for delivery to be completed, accepted and paid for. Thus the customer needs to perform a long-stop quality assurance: an ultimate 'no' if the correct procedures are not followed, tests are not performed exactly as planned, if all problems are not fully cleared and if documentation is not up-to-date.

When the software for Spacelab was completed, I moved to the Technical Directorate to take up a quality assurance role. As well as the usual concerns about standards and procedures, I wanted to develop a more general software engineering approach, and promote better technology. To this end, I first became interested in Ada in 1982, before Ada was standardised. It seemed obvious that Ada would be a good language for ESA projects since Ada was being designed specifically for embedded software, which is a major part of ESA's software, and that a lot of effort was going into Ada and producing a language which combined new and old software engineering concepts. On the other hand, critics saw a language that was too heavy, that was 'not adapted for real time', for which no validated compilers were available for a long time, and for which no industrial quality compilers were available for even longer.

ESA Technical Directorate runs a technical research program each year, of which software is a small part. In 1985, Michel Guerin, then head of the Simulation Section of the Mathematics Division of Estec, decided to investigate the feasibility of using Ada by starting a small study in which an existing piece of operational software, in fact an attitude control system written in assembler, would be rewritten in Ada along with its accompanying simulation test environment, written in Fortran. ESA re-programmed the onboard software into Ada, using mainly the Program Design Language (PDL) provided as a design, and the industrial contractors reprogrammed the Fortran simulation into Ada. The resulting software was then run on a Data General system and produced the correct results, although rather more slowly than the corresponding Fortran simulation. The conclusion was that Ada would work, but would not be usable for operational software at that time, and that Ada would not take over from Fortran on existing projects or on existing application types for some considerable time.

In 1986, the Mathematics Division decided that if Ada were to be used, then ESA would need to know how to design Ada software, and so a study contract was awarded jointly to three companies (CISI Ingenierie (France), Matra Espace (France) and CRI A/S (Denmark)) to evaluate existing design methods for suitability, if necessary to produce a new method, and to develop a training course. The result is HOOD, which was completed in 1987.

When HOOD had been defined and the training course was being completed, it was clear that if European Space Industry were to accept HOOD as a suitable method, then a computer aided software engineering (CASE) toolset would be needed to enforce the method as well as facilitating its use. The HOOD toolset would aid the designer in the difficult task of producing and maintaining the graphics easily, and would support the formal aspects, including checking of HOOD rules. This would therefore meet the management need for consistency and productivity, and the quality assurance needs for quality and correctness.

In 1988, a contract was awarded to Software Sciences in the UK, with support from CISI Ingenierie, Matra Espace and CRI A/S, to develop a HOOD toolset according to the ESA Software Engineering Standards PSS-05-0. In 1988, the Columbus Space Station project adopted HOOD for the architectural design phase, and in 1989 Hermes Spaceplane project also selected HOOD. As a result of this interest, other companies developed toolsets with varying technologies, but all following the standard method.

During 1989, the HOOD Working Group took account of comments about HOOD from the first users, and the need for new features to update the *HOOD Reference Manual* to Issue 3.0, and to produce the *HOOD User Manual*. ESA was keen to avoid disturbing designers, contractors and tool vendors during the early design phase, and decided not to change HOOD again for at least three years. ESA, therefore, withdrew from the development of HOOD, passing control to the HOOD User Group, which had been initiated in the first contract for the definition of HOOD.

HOOD has since been adopted by several military projects in Europe, notably the European Fighter Aircraft, by a nuclear power monitoring project in Belgium, by French electricity projects, and a large communication network project. It is fair to say that, in Europe, HOOD is considered for most major Ada projects as an established method well supported by CASE tools.

1.1.2 ESA software engineering life-cycle

HOOD was initially developed to fit into the ESA software engineering life-cycle which consists of the following phases and may be presented in the classic V shape in Figure 1.1.

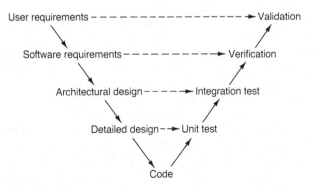

Figure 1.1 ESA software engineering life-cycle.

This life-cycle is primarily directed to an independent piece of software, that has a user to define the requirements in a User Requirements Document. For an embedded system, the user requirements are replaced by system requirements, subsystem requirements or equipment requirements, which define the requirements for a combined piece of hardware and software. In any case, the next step is to isolate the software requirements in a Software Requirements Document (SRD). Generally, this is produced by a contractor in a consortium, led by a prime contractor. After this SRD has been reviewed and approved by technical, quality assurance and managerial staff from the prime contractor and the agency, the design work can begin. The architectural design is intended to show the overall structure of the proposed design, whereas the detailed design is required to provide a sufficiently detailed description of the design to allow coding to follow. Both the Architectural Design Document and the Detailed Design Document are reviewed and revised to check conformance with the documented requirements. The software is then coded, and is first tested in units using the detailed design as the requirements for the test cases. The purpose of the integration test is to show that the completed software is consistent with the architectural design, with particular emphasis on testing interfaces between code components, and on external interfaces. Verification is carried out to demonstrate that the integrated software completely satisfies all the requirements documented in the SRD, and validation is performed to demonstrate that the software meets the documented user's requirements and that the software will operate successfully.

In an ideal world, the SRD is the starting point for HOOD. In practice, the requirements are not usually complete and unchanging at this stage. Often the hardware requirements are unclear because the hardware itself is also under development in a similar but parallel life-cycle. Thus the theoretical approach has to be read and understood to be carried out in a less than ideal environment. This means that changes should be expected, that top-down does not have to be applied rigidly, and that it is the principles of the method that are important. There is, therefore, still a role for the human being as software designer. In Chapter 10, we look at the interface to requirements, mainly to consider how requirements could better be defined to support the design phase.

One of the major objectives of the architectural design is to provide a clear identification of the components of the design and their interfaces. Such architectures are most clearly expressed using good diagrams, especially data flow and control flow diagrams. ESA experience was that contractors were generally unwilling to commit themselves to an architectural design until the detailed design was complete, and probably preferred to have completed coding. There was a hint of a suspicion that really coding was coming before design. Accordingly, good diagrams were to be an important part of HOOD.

HOOD does not stop there, though. In fact, a good HOOD toolset takes the designer right through the Detailed Design phase into coding and testing, by providing a text-based format for each object which can be refined step by step from a bare description of the functionality and operational interfaces, to a pseudocode definition, to full code in the desired target language, i.e. Ada. Since most HOOD designers do the programming as well, this is eminently sensible. There is therefore no real break in the implementation from architecture to code. Currently, the break in the life-cycle is between requirements and design: between statement of the problem and development of the solution. Again, Chapter 10 looks into ways of reducing this break by providing an object life-cycle.

As a consequence, one may say that HOOD is not just an isolated method, but is a large part of the software development process. This is apparent when HOOD is extended to include requirement references for each object, thus allowing a requirement/object cross-reference table to be developed and maintained. Another approach, which is used in the Columbus Software Development Environment (SDE) for example, is to provide a relational database, which includes requirements and traces to HOOD objects. The SDE, which is an example of an integrated programming support environment (IPSE), is also used to provide configuration management, not only of HOOD objects and designs, but also of all the other documentation and code; this is the reason why HOOD does not provide any specific configuration management features.

1.1.3 Ada design method development

The purpose of the contract let by ESA in 1986/7 was to develop an Ada-oriented design method, supported by a training course, with the following additional constraints:

1. The new method had to be acceptable to a wide range of European companies, some with existing methods, and some without. It could not therefore easily be an existing national method unless this could be shown to be excellent. The experience of real-time programming languages, where Coral was developed and used in the UK, Pearl in Germany and LTR (Langage Temps Réele) in France, but each language was not accepted by other countries, was to be avoided.
2. The method should be suitable for developing software for large systems, so that they can be developed by multiple contractors in different sites and then integrated to form a complete system.
3. The method should be adaptable for software systems to run on multiple computers – these two points lead to an emphasis on interface definition and on software integration.
4. The method should follow Structured Analysis and Design Technique (SADT) and English definition of requirements since SADT was the method being considered at that stage for requirements and was being used by the French Space Agency CNES. In fact, the SADT aspect is not specifically addressed by HOOD, although the *User Manual* looks into this point.
5. The method should lead onto Program Design Language (PDL) in the Detailed Design phase, and to Ada for coding: this is seen in the formal structure of the

text form used in the later stages of the design, complemented by pseudocode which may be transformed in the Detailed Design into PDL or Ada. Since Ada is high level language, the use of PDL or pseudocode has less added value than it would have for an assembler-level language. On the other hand, a formal definition of the object has value at the design stage, providing a slightly more rigid structure than a programming language generally does. A formal language could also be used in this way.

1.1.4 Shortlist of methods

Several of the design methods that existed in 1987 were looked at:

1. Top-down functional decomposition methods such as Yourdon and structured analysis/structured design (SA/SD) were seen as process-oriented methods that did not lead naturally into Ada, and lacked features of concurrency that would be needed.
2. Data structure driven methods such as Jackson Structured Design (JSD) were thought to be too data-oriented for embedded systems, which are often event-driven.
3. SADT was seen as being useful for analysis but not so suitable for design, but simpler than data flow diagrams in structured analysis.
4. Petri nets were identified as being good for the real-time aspects of a design, but inadequate for the design as a whole. The Columbus project intends to use petri nets for the detailed design of the real-time aspects of HOOD objects.
5. Mascot-3 was not fully available at that time, and Mascot-2 was thought to be inadequate for Ada.
6. Auto-G was considered to be too detailed for architecture design (i.e. lacking the data flow and control aspects), and very dependent on one supplier, thus imposing a high risk.

On the other hand, three methods were thought to be suitable and synthesised into HOOD:

1. Object-oriented design, as defined by Grady Booch and widely accepted for Ada, offered a good mapping into Ada and a valuable approach but was seen as lacking a method prescription fo large systems, since it seemed to be used only at the top level.
2. Abstract machines provided a good but rigid structure, and were being used by companies in France, including Matra Espace.
3. Ada-based PDL could be used for the more detailed aspects: there were already some PDLs (e.g. ANNA – ANNotated Ada) but without good pre-processing tools at that time.

Thus HOOD was developed to formalise object-oriented design into a method, and to build object hierarchies, supported by a formal textual definition for later refinement into code. Time has, to some extent, validated these decisions.

1.2 RATIONALE FOR THE HOOD APPROACH

HOOD is based on software engineering principles of abstraction, encapsulation and modularity, and is built into the standard software development life-cycle as embodied in the ESA software engineering standards. Although HOOD is, therefore, described primarily as a top-down method, particularly suitable for a project development environment, HOOD also provides a suitable framework for a domain development approach, and provides useful features for maintenance, both enhancement and correction.

As a result of the synthesis of object-oriented design (OOD) with abstract machines, and the introduction of hierarchical decomposition, HOOD includes the following software engineering features:

- *Abstraction.* The facility to deal with complexity by focusing on the important elements of the problem. At the top level of the design, the objects are at a higher level of abstraction: that is, these objects relate to each other and provide a complete solution to the problem without a great deal of detail. The lower-level objects are not visible. This is hierarchical decomposition. The design is shown in such a way that the structure and interfaces are clear and separated from the details of the processing. Emphasis is made on the control flows and data flows at an early stage, using diagrams to show these, along with the object interfaces.

  An example of abstraction is that of the management of a disk-based system, where a file is the top-level abstraction, a disk is the next level, a sector another level, and the device driver the bottom level (Figure 1.2).
- *Information hiding.* The essence of an object is that the data are encapsulated inside the object, and are accessible only through external operations. This is

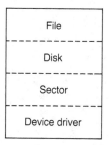

Figure 1.2 Levels of abstraction.

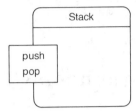

Figure 1.3 Object **stack**.

strongly supported by Ada (specification and body), although not enforced
(data are allowed to be visible in the specification part). Details of the
implementation are hidden in the body of the object (also called *encapsulation*). An example is a stack object which provides operations to pop and push
data onto the stack while maintaining the stack itself hidden in the stack object,
i.e. the data representation of the stack is in the Ada package body Figure 1.3).

■ *Locality or cohesion.* To aid maintenance, abstractions that are logically
related are also physically related, i.e. the data and code related to an entity are
in the same object or package. Thus if a change is required by a change to the
environment, then the effects on the software are localised. For example, if an
object is used to manage a screen, with a defined set of operations, then if the
hardware is changed and requires detailed changes to the software, the
operational software interface of the object may remain unchanged so that the
rest of the software system is not affected.

■ *Modularity.* The software is split into many components, each clearly defined,
and clearly related to other entities either by control flow or by decomposition.

These software engineering features support the HOOD abilities of:

■ *Maintainability*
   · The software is easier to understand through separation of structure and
     detail.
   · Software documentation is easy to read through structured documentation
     according to objects.
   · There is a clear mapping from problem to design solution.
   · There is a clear mapping from design to code, supported by HOOD being
     specifically designed for Ada.
■ *Reusability*
   · Because of the strong relation of applicability to the real world, objects can
     be reused whenever the corresponding real world entity is required, i.e. in
     similar applications.
   · Objects related to data entities can be reused in other programs in the
     application suite related to those data entities, e.g. a record structure for a
     file, a message or a command.

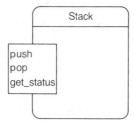

Figure 1.4 Object **stack** extended.

- An object may be of a more general nature, and therefore may be reused in a new configuration, e.g. list and stack objects.
■ *Configurability*
  - An object may be parameterised (e.g. use of a class).
  - An object may be replaced by another object with the same interface, but supporting a different hardware or software configuration.
■ *Extensibility*
  - Operations may be added to an existing object (e.g. an extra function 'get_ status' can easily be added to an object **stack** (Figure 1.4).
  - An object may be reused in a new design, encapsulated into another object that extends the functionality, which looks like inheritance due to mapping the operational interface to a higher level.
■ *Productivity*
  - Reuse across a project leads to increased productivity in initial development, while subsequent new developments of similar applications may benefit to a much greater extent.
  - Ada has already shown great productivity gains in the software integration phase due to early validation of interfaces and package robustness. HOOD carries this approach into the design phases.

The HOOD method is most easily described as a top-down, project oriented method. However, it is also important to remember that many projects do not lend themselves easily to this rather idealistic approach. In many cases, the top-level requirements are not clear at the beginning of software development, so it may be necessary to begin by identifying and developing lower-level objects, nearer to the hardware, thus developing a library of objects that can be later incorporated into the design. This may also be described as providing a virtual machine layer on which to develop the actual application when the requirements are known. This is shown in Figure 1.5.

On the other hand, the overall requirements may be known but the hardware still under development. In this case, the top-down approach allows only the interfaces of lower-level objects to be defined, leaving dummy stub objects to be used for initial testing.

Finally, the application domain approach, which is recommended for object-

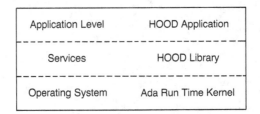

Figure 1.5 Software layers.

oriented systems, is perhaps the ideal that is rarely achievable. In this technique, the domain of the applications that are the designer's responsibility is searched, and suitable objects are identified and developed into code. Thus whenever an application is required, the infrastructure of useful objects is available. This technique requires investment ahead of project approval, and may lead to a clearer vision of which objects may be most useful for reuse. Few of us, however, are allowed this luxury, working in an environment where funding is provided specifically for projects. Consequently, it is likely to be more feasible to remember the potential for reuse during development of a project, and to put suitable objects developed during the course of a project into a library as a basis of an application domain library for subsequent reuse.

2

HOOD METHOD

2.1 DESIGN PROCESS

The HOOD method is primarily top-down. It consists of a Basic Design Step, which is applied to the program at the top level to transform the program into a top-level set of objects, and is then applied successively to each object until a set of terminal objects is reached, none of which can usefully be decomposed further.

However, HOOD could equally well be used to develop a design reusing existing objects, partly top-down and partly bottom-up. When the overall requirements of a project are not known at the start of software development (it does happen), it may be possible to start by developing some lower-level objects, perhaps associated with the user interface, special hardware or data storage, in order to provide an initial set of objects that can be fully tested and developed, ready to be integrated into the design when the project requirements are defined. In embedded systems, it is often the case that the hardware is being developed in parallel with the software, so that the opposite is true, i.e. the general top-level requirements are known, but the hardware is evolving, so that the bottom-level objects that interface to the hardware are being revised continually revised as the hardware changes. In this case, the lower-level objects provide an insulating layer to allow the top-level objects to be developed while being kept out of range of these detailed changes. Whichever design process is used, the resulting design will consist of a set of objects which are a hierarchical decomposition of the program into a constituent set of interdependent objects.

This process of successive decomposition results in a HOOD design tree (Figure 2.1), in which the program being designed is represented by a root object from which the tree of hierarchically decomposed objects depends. Each object that is decomposed into others is called a parent object, and it may be fully replaced by its child objects. So a parent object is, in effect, an empty shell object serving primarily to provide an architecture to the system.

Thus we may say that the program as a whole consists entirely of the set of objects at the first level; and each of these objects at the first level can be represented by a further set of objects at the second level. Interactions between objects at the first level are in fact implemented by objects at the second, or even subsequent levels. This gives rise to what is called an uncle object, where there is an interaction between a child object and another object at the level of its parent object, called an uncle object. This is explained more fully in Chapter 4, section 4.5.

Each of the terminal objects is then implemented by defining the logic of each of its operations in pseudocode, and then in the target language Ada, together with the types, data, constants, exceptions and other internal operations needed to support the implementation of the object and its interface. A HOOD design can thus be modelled by this HOOD design tree (HDT), with several design levels, where upper level objects correspond to higher abstractions, and lower-level objects are closer to programming abstractions.

Figure 2.1 gives an abstract example of such HDT. This figure shows the root object, representing the system to design, at the top level of the tree (i.e. with no parent object). The design process may follow the graph shown as follows:

Design level 1

- Step 0 produces objects obj_1, obj_2, obj_3, obj_4.

Design level 2

- Step 1 produces objects O11, O12, O13.
- Step 2 produces objects O21, O22.

Design level 3

- Step 3, step 4, step 5 and so on.

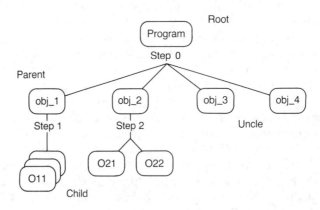

Top-down in Basic Design Steps

Figure 2.1 HOOD design tree.

Each object, except the root object, is completely defined through two successive design steps:

1. At level $i - 1$: an object is identified as a child object of the level above, and is partially specified through a first refinement to define its interfaces.
2. At level i: either the object is considered as a parent object and is decomposed into child objects, allowing a complete, validated Object Description Skeleton (ODS) to be produced, or the object is seen to be a terminal object and the details of the design are completed.

The general diagram of a HOOD design tree shows, therefore, the ROOT object decomposed in the first design step into child objects obj_1, obj_2, obj_3 and obj_4. Step 2 could then decompose object obj_1 into objects O11, O12 and O13. Object obj_2 could then be designed, followed by objects obj_3 and obj_4. Thus the design process continues across all the objects at the same level. This has the benefit of validating the first design step, and providing immediate feedback to the first-level decompostion.

However, if it is preferred, it is also a good design approach to continue to decompose down one branch of the tree. Thus object obj_1 could be decomposed until terminal objects are reached before moving onto objects obj_2 and obj_3. This second approach would be necessary, and run concurrently, when a team is allocated to each of the limbs. It would probably be the approach adopted in a large project. However, the preferred option is to decompose level by level since this provides an earlier degree of checking back to the top level for consistency.

For example, it may be that at one level of decomposition, one or more operations that are needed in the design are not identified in the first pass, but are identified at the next level. An earlier opportunity is then given to go back to the first level and to add an extra operation.

As an example of a HOOD design tree, let us consider a simple text editor, in which commands and text are entered from a keyboard, and the composed text is output to a screen, and stored in a file. Figure 2.2 shows a possible first level of decomposition.

The text object shall hold a block of text, and provide operations to insert text into a paragraph, reformat a paragraph, display a page, etc. The text object may be therefore be decomposed further into objects, as shown in Figures 2.3 and 2.4.

The decomposition process will be developed further in this and other chapters.

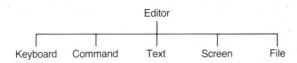

Figure 2.2 HDT for editor.

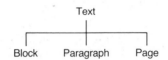

Figure 2.3 HDT for text.

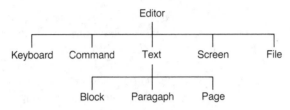

Figure 2.4 Full HDT for editor.

2.2 THE BASIC DESIGN STEP

The top-down hierarchical decomposition approach is not new. After all, this is the method used with data flow diagrams starting from a context diagram which shows all the external interfaces with one central process. This process is then decomposed into other processes with data flows and control flows interacting between them, with consistency checks between levels. In the same way, the purpose of HOOD is to develop the design as a set of obects which together provide the functionality of the program. In the next chapter, we go into more detail on what an object is and how we find objects. At this stage, we are concerned mainly with the overall method for developing the design.

A Basic Design Step has as its goal the identification of child objects of a given parent object, and of their individual relationships to other existing objects, or the refinement of a terminal object to the level of the code. This process is based on the identification of obects by means of object-oriented design techniques which are described more fully in Chapter 3.

A Basic Design Step is split into four phases, thus defining a micro life-cycle for the design of each object. The phases can be summarised as follows (see also Figure 2.5):

1. Problem definition.
2. Development of solution strategy.
3. Formalisation of the strategy.
4. Formalisation of the solution.

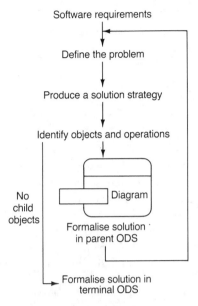

Software requirements

Define the problem

Produce a solution strategy

Identify objects and operations

No child objects

Diagram

Formalise solution
in parent ODS

Formalise solution in
terminal ODS

ODS object description skeleton

Figure 2.5 Basic Design Step.

2.2.1 Phase 1. Problem definition

Phase 1. Problem definition

The context of the object to be designed is stated, with the goal of organising and structuring the data from the requirement analysis phase. This is an opportunity to provide a completeness check on requirements and traceability to design.

The description of the problem to be solved is made up of two parts:

1.1 *Statement of the problem.* The designer provides a set of references to the software requirements documents for the program or object. If there is no suitable requirement documentation, the designer states the problem in correct sentences which provide:
· a clear and precise definition of the problem;
· the context of the system to design.
This may not be easy in practice.

1.2 *Analysis and structuring of requirement data.* This subphase is the key point of
the Basic Design Step activities. The purpose of this analysis is to make sure
that the problem has been well understood. Thus the designer gathers and
analyses all the information relevant to the problem, including the environment of the system to be designed.

One way to proceed is to separate the requirements (already collected in the
software requirement phase) into different types, mapped as follows:

- Static functional requirements used to:
  - · Identify objects.
  - · Define the process to be done which will be reflected in the definition of the
    operations in the HOOD Operation Control Structures (OPCS).
- Dynamic functional requirements used to:
  - · Identify type of object.
  - · Describe the dynamic behaviour of the system (when and under what
    conditions processing is to take place). These may be specified in petri nets
    or state transition diagrams, and are incorporated in the Object Control
    Structures (OBCS).
- Non-functional requirements, which may be described in the ODS implemen-
  tation or synchronisation constraints.

If the requirement analysis work has already been done fully in an earlier phase of the
software life-cycle, this section can reference the relevant document without
repeating the work in this HOOD step.

2.2.2 Phase 2. Development of solution strategy

Phase 2. Development of solution strategy

The outline solution of the problem stated above is described in terms of
objects at a high level of abstraction.

The goal of this phase is to create an outline solution of the problem that has been
defined. This solution is descibed by using a natural language explaining how the
design works for the current level of abstraction. At the top level, this solution
should describe the design by means of real-world objects and be associated with
the actions which may be performed on them.

This solution should not be considered as definitive, but as a baseline for further
refinement in the following phase of the Basic Design Step. The method for
describing the design is elaborated in Chapter 3.

2.2.3 Phase 3. Formalisation of the strategy

Phase 3. Formalisation of the strategy

The objects and their associated operations are defined. A HOOD diagram of the proposed design solution is produced, allowing easy visualisation of the concepts and further formalisation.

This phase has as its goal the extraction of the major concepts of the solution strategy in order to come smoothly to a formalised description of the solution in diagrammatic form. If the informal description cannot be formalised, it may be because the solution strategy is incomplete; in this case it is recommended to repeat phase 2.

There are five subphases in the formalisation of the strategy:

3.1 *Object identification*. The designer identifies the objects by extracting nouns from the solution strategy. The designer must identify and structure these nouns according to their behaviour and their associated level of abstraction (e.g. a noun may represent an object which is not relevant to the design at the current level of abstraction). The result of this phase is a list of each identified noun, assigned as a child object, an attribute of an object, a value of an attribute or as a redundant 'noise' word, with a corresponding textual description. This is stored as the *object identification*. If no new objects are found, then this object is in fact a terminal object, and is not decomposed further. Refinement of the detailed design continues in phase 4.

3.2 *Operation identification*. The designer identifies the operations by means of the same mechanism as in subphase 3.1, but this time the verbs are extracted from the solution strategy. All properties, related to the operation execution (i.e. parallelism, synchronisation, periodic execution), should also be reported in this phase. The result of this phase is a list and textual description of each identified operation. This is stored as the *operation identification*.

3.3 *Grouping objects and operations (object operation table)*. Each operation is then associated with an object. This grouping gives a structured representation of the strategy and helps to establish a formal description of the objects as well as leading to a graphical description of the solution. The outcome of this phase is the list of the objects with each associated operation, called the *object operation table* or OOT.

Steps 3.2 and 3.3 have separated the objects and the corresponding operations which were together in the solution strategy; this step simply regroups them to provide a clear definition of the objects and their corresponding operations as input to the next Basic Design Step.

3.4 *Graphical description*. Using the HOOD graphical formalism, the designer produces a diagram corresponding to the solution outlined in the strategy. The first version includes the objects and operations identified in the object operation table described in 3.3, i.e. this diagram identifies the child objects into which the parent object is decomposed. The designer then adds control flow dependencies between objects, expressing the way in which each object uses operations of the other child objects, and adds corresponding major data flows and exception flows to express the relationships between the child objects. Lastly, the designer adds a mapping from each operation of the parent object onto the corresponding child object that implements the functionality of the parent object.

In order to define the design completely, the designer may also use different types of object, such as active objects to provide concurrency, class and instance objects to provide genericity, environment objects to interface to existing software, or software being developed externally. Software being designed to run on a multiprocessor system may also be designed using virtual node objects (VNs), which provide the flexibility of allowing objects to be allocated to a processor later in the design process when resource use and budgets have been refined.

The details of the formalisms of the HOOD diagram are described in Chapter 4.

3.5 *Justification of design decisions.* When a design decision has been made, it is documented by the designer, who explains the reasons for the decision, for the benefit of a design reviewer or for a maintainer in the future. In general, a justification is required for the choice of object type for those objects which are neither passive nor environment objects. In the same way, a justification is needed for each of those operations which are constrained. As a design goal, the number of active objects should be minimised, consistent with the requirements of the software, to reduce the tasking complexity and to reduce the task-switching overheads. A justification is also required for each exception that is identified, since an exception is potentially a hazardous incursion into the control flow.

The formalisation of the strategy (phase 3) may lead to several iterations of the development of the solution strategy (phase 2), until a sufficient understanding of the solution has been reached, and a consistent set of sections has been defined.

2.2.4 Phase 4. Formalisation of the solution

Phase 4. Formalisation of the solution

The solution is formalised through formal definition of Provided object interfaces and formal description of Object and Operation Control Structures.

When the formalisation of the strategy has been completed, the designer can elaborate a formal model of the solution, describing for each parent object the properties of each of its child objects, the interface declaration and logic of each operation, and the relationship among the child objects. This model is called the Object Description Skeleton (ODS), which is described fully in Chapter 5.

The capture of this formal description consists in filling in each field of the Object Description Skeleton. For each object, the ODS may be considered in two parts – the Visible part and the Internals – with the following contents:

Visible part
- Object-level information, such as type of object and a description of the object.
- A formal description of the interfaces of the object.
- A description of the Object Control Structure which defines the synchronisation and relationships between constrained operations of an active obect.
- A list of data flows and exception flows to and from this object.

Internals
- A definition of the internal child objects, types, constants, operations and data.
- The Object Control Structure detailed design.
- A formal description of the Operation Control Structure for each Provided or Internal operation of the object.
- Informal comments may be added at any point to describe the semantic behaviour, to provide useful information for further implementation or to justify implementation decisions.

At the end of this phase, the ODS of the object is fully and formally described. From now on it will remain the source of documentation for detailed design and code generation. The design structure may be turned automatically into an Ada package and task structure from the ODS. Its usefulness and compilability depend on whether the content of the ODS conforms to Ada language.

When this refinement process is complete, each object is then reviewed in turn.

One of the key features of HOOD is to provide strong definition of the interfaces of each object at an early stage in the design process, so that the interfaces can be checked and held to be consistent throughout the design phases. An important part of the interface control is the relationship between objects, both the decomposition from parent to child and also between objects at the same level.

2.3 APPLICATION OF THE BASIC DESIGN STEP

Although the Basic Design Step is, in principle, applied to all objects, there are detailed differences in the way that it can be applied to root and terminal objects.

2.3.1 Root object

Unlike the other objects, the root object is completely defined through one Basic Design Step, since it is always the parent object of the program. Thus the goals of the Basic Design Step appertaining to the root object are:

1. To define the interfaces of the root object.
2. To identify its child objects and their relationships.

The impacts on the four phases of the Basic Design Step are, in outline:

- *Phase 1. Problem definition.* The designer gathers and analyses all information relevant to the program to be designed with respect to the level of abstraction. Moreover, the designer puts the emphasis on the interfaces of the program, and of the environment of the Program To Design (PTD). It may be useful to show a context diagram of the program within its environment.
- *Phase 2. Development of a solution strategy.* This phase follows the general scheme described in section 2.2.2.
- *Phase 3. Formalisation of the strategy.* The process of identification of operations applies to the operations of the root object itself. Therefore the output of subphase 3.3 should also contain a list of associated Provided operations for the root object. The graphical description should show:
  · the root object and its operations
  · the relevant environment objects
  · the different child objects and their associated operations
  · all the Use relationships, Implemented_by links, the dataflows, exceptions, etc.
- *Phase 4. Formalisation of the solution.* All relevant fields of the Object Description Skeleton are completed in the way described in section 2.2.4. Each operation of a root object will be implemented by a child operation.

There is a view that the root object does not need to provide any operations: that the root object is a special case, and may be seen to represent the program itself and execute directly. However, this does not provide design by successive decomposition, and does not show the full interface of the design at the top level – useful to give a clear view of the design.

On the other hand, the root object be seen to be 'just another object' which happens to be the root of this particular design, but might be reused in another program as a part of a hierarchy. Indeed, when a design is subcontracted to several teams or companies, each subhierarchy will temporarily have a root object for its part of the design for that contractor. It is an important point in HOOD that all interfaces should be fully defined early in the design process, and so only a real top-level root can reasonably avoid having Provided operations in general. This is discussed further in Chapter 4, section 4.2.

2.3.2 Terminal object

The Basic Design Step applied to the terminal objects is shorter and each phase is restricted as follows:

- *Phase 1. Problem definition.* The designer should gather all the information related to the object in the normal way.
- *Phase 2. Development of a solution strategy.* The solution strategy is developed in the normal way. If the identification of objects reveals no new objects, then the object is seen to be terminal. The purpose of this phase is, therefore, to provide a description of the terminal object in order to define the behaviour of the object, and the process or function of each operation, i.e. the OBCS and OPCS(s) of the object. Further internal operations ay be identified during expansion of the description of the solution strategy for the object.
- *Phase 3. Formalisation of the strategy.* Since no child object is identified, the first parts of this phase are not applicable to a terminal object. However, it is useful to produce the diagram of the object, with its object type, its Provided operations and relationship to other objects as documentation of the object, both for reviewers in this design and for the benefit of potential future designers wanting to reuse the object in other designs.
- *Phase 4. Formalisation of the solution.* This phase follows the general scheme defined in section 2.2.4.

The designer should first review the library of existing objects to see if another object already exists that can be reused, possibly with extension or minor modification. If the changes needed are extensive, and the object is needed in the library as it is, it may be necessary to copy an existing object, rename it and then modify it. Or it may be possible to modify the object by extending the Provided interface, or other parts, and return it to the library with a new version number.

The designer should then review the library of existing class objects to see if a class object exists from which an instance object can be made to meet the needs of this object. Again it may be necessary to modify a class object to make it completely suitable. In an object-oriented programming language, such an extension would be done by creating a new class that inherits the old class and adds functionality to it.

If neither of these reuse possibilites is suitable, then the logic of each operation is defined in three stages:

1. A description in natural language.
2. A design in pseudocode.
3. The Ada source code.

2.4 HOOD CHAPTER SKELETON

One of the main benefits of a standard development method is that a corresponding standard form of documentation can be produced. This is of obvious benefit to a designer using a CASE tool who has simply to press a button to produce beautifully formatted and tailored documentation from all the design data stored by his or her CASE tool. Each of the phases of the Basic Design Step produces a text unit, a diagram or a structured text unit (ODS or Ada).

A standard HOOD document is equally of value to managers, who can be sure of getting documentation easily with no manpower overhead, to quality assurance, who can be sure that documentation standards are followed and that the documentation is consistent with the design, and to the customer or reviewer who will receive a document which looks familiar, with everything in its place. The biggest benefit, though, is to the maintainer, who can be sure that the document that he or she has does reflect the code that has been produced.

For HOOD, then, the Basic Design Step process is documented by means of a HOOD chapter for each object developed according to a standard format called a HOOD Chapter Skeleton (HCS). The goal of the HOOD chapter is to provide a complete object description, which may be reviewed and further refined in the Detailed Design and Coding phases of the software engineering life-cycle.

The chapters of the HCS have subsections which correspond to the Basic Design Step phases for each object:

HOOD Chapter Skeleton

1   Problem definition
    1.1 Problem statement
    1.2 Requirement analysis

2   Informal solution strategy

3   Formalisation of the strategy
    3.1 Object identification
    3.2 Operation identification
    3.3 Object operation table
    3.4 Graphical description
    3.5 Justification of design decisions

4   Formalisation of the solution
    4.1 Object description skeleton
    4.2 Generated Ada source code

A HOOD document may be created as a set of HOOD chapters structured according to the HOOD design tree. There is one HOOD chapter per object. In addition, text relating to the design as a whole may be added by the designer or generated automatically by a CASE tool. For example, a front cover page, an introduction and appendices with cross-references about the design may be added.

The HOOD Chapter Skeleton definition represents guidelines for the HOOD document production, which may be adapted according to the needs of the project or designer. For example, the HOOD chapter subsections may be used to produce different types of document:

- Architectural Design Document (ADD) from sections 1, 2, 3 and pseudocode ODS (4.1).
- Detailed Design Document (DDD) from sections 1, 2, subsection 3.4 and full ODS (4.1).
- Ada source code from 1.1, 3.4 and 4.2.

A particular example is that the Ada code may not be needed for the Architectural Design review, but could be included for the Detailed Design review, possibly in a separate document.

A document may be printed for the whole design, for one object, or for a subtree of objects. In this way, a HOOD document of an object provides a complete design definition of the object, including its interfaces, so that a library of HOOD documents could provide the designer with a means of assessing whether any existing object is suitable for the design. This constitutes a library of objects for reuse.

Alternatively the designer may consider the Object Description Skeleton as the basis for the HOOD document, since the ODS contains all the details of the design, and therefore the HOOD diagram can be generated from the ODS. In that case, each part of the HOOD chapter may be included in the Object Description Skeleton of the parent object. This technique is used in the Standard Interchange Format (SIF) which has been defined to provide a means of transferring a design from one CASE tool to another, and so to provide portability of designs between CASE tools from different vendors or between different computer platforms on which the tool may be running. The SIF is defined in the *HOOD Reference Manual Issue 3.1*, Appendix E.

The contents of each section of a HOOD chapter may be summarised as follows:

1. *Problem definition*. This chapter needs to have sufficient detail to define the problem, without solving it. If there is a good Software Requirements Document, then references to the SRD are better than simple repetition of text. A data flow diagram and state transition diagram may be used to supplement the text.
2. *Informal solution strategy*. The solution strategy is a key chapter, generally produced before the diagram, describing the proposed solution in natural language. From it the objects and operations can be identified, either as real-world objects, or as software type objects related to data entities.

3. *Formalisation of the strategy.* This chapter lists, describes and relates the objects and operations from the solution strategy, as a preparatory step to developing the HOOD diagram. The HOOD diagram provides a user-friendly view of the decomposition of the design into objects, including data flows and control flows (Use relationships). Justification of design decisions is especially applicable to selection of active objects and exceptions.

4. *Formalisation of the solution.* The Object Description Skeleton provides a formal definition of the design of the object, derived from the diagram, which can be checked for completeness, internal consistency and interface coherence. The ODS can be used to transfer the design to another platform or toolset, to generate Ada source code, or to generate HOOD diagrams as a reverse process for designs copied from another toolset or platform.

Ada generated from the ODS may be used initially for prototyping, and may be refined to produce the final implementation. The Ada source is not needed in the Architectural Design Document, but it may appear in the Detailed Design Document if required by the project standards, or simply remain in the Ada source code library.

3

FINDING OBJECTS AND OPERATIONS

The purpose of the HOOD designer is to turn a definition of the requirements into a set of software objects, that are combined to form one or more programs. In Chapter 2 we looked at the HOOD method as a whole. In this chapter, we will start by developing a definition of an object and look at ways of finding objects, both by the standard HOOD approach and then more directly from requirements defined in more formal ways such as data flow diagrams.

3.1 OBJECT DEFINITION

HOOD begins with the assumption that the requirements have been defined in a Software Requirements Document (SRD) or in another equivalent document, often called a specification of some form. In some projects, the word 'specification' is used variously for requirements and design, which may be confusing. This assumption will always be true to a greater or lesser extent in order for design work to proceed with some authority. If you are asked to produce a design without a written Software Requirements Document, then you would be well advised to compile one, formally or informally, in order to separate the statement of the problem to be solved from the means by which it is to be achieved. This does not, however, imply that a HOOD designer should naively assume that requirements will not change during the design and implementation process, nor that the requirements are necessarily well defined, clear and unambiguous. This assumption is simply a statement of the basis from which HOOD proceeds.

The Software Requirements Document may be in any form, either the Columbus standard of SADT and related English text, or the European Fighter Aircraft project standard of Controlled Requirement Expression (CORE) and/or BPOS, or more commonly in Yourdon structured analysis diagrams (SA). Additional possibilities are entity relation diagrams (ERD), state transition diagrams (STD) and petri nets.

3.1.1 Definition of an object

There are many sources for a definition of object, but in the context of object oriented design for Ada software, the most relevant are the books of Grady Booch. One may see an evolution in the definitions, from an emphasis on real-world entities to a more software-oriented position. Thus an early quote is:

> [in] the problem space we have some real world objects, each of which has a set of appropriate operations.
>
> *(Software Engineering in Ada*, 1983, p.38)

This definition emphasises the external-world aspects of an object, which are paramount at the top level of decomposition where the problem statement is generally in terms of real-world hardware or application files. It also points to the combination aspect of operations on an object, leading to encapsulation of the data within an object thus allowing access only through operations on those data, either to change the data or to provide the data in some way.

In *Software Components with Ada* (p.20), Grady Booch gives the following definition:

> An *object* is an entity that
> · has state,
> · is characterised by the actions that it suffers and that it requires of other objects,
> · is a unique instance of some (possibly anonymous) class,
> · is denoted by a name,
> · has restricted visibility of and by other objects,
> · can be viewed either by its specification or by its implementation.

This definition introduces the concept of the state of an object. This is a particularly important source for a controlling object, which might reflect the system state (in a general sense, a system might have states such as 'uninitialised', 'normal', 'error' and 'close-down'), and for a concurrent object that interacts with other objects and needs to retain knowledge of the overall 'state' of the system. State is also present in the sense of stored data as well as a control state.

This definition also emphasises the relationships between objects, that an object in isolation has no value, but that a system is made up of objects that interact through the operations on them.

The idea of class is also introduced by this definition: every object may be seen as a named case of a more general definition called a class. However, this is not necessarily helpful for much of the software which is specific but is useful where commonality can be introduced in the same way as the Ada generic package.

The name of the object is a good pointer to the quality of the object: if it cannot be easily named, then it is probably not a good object. Restricted visibility of other objects is part of the structure of the software design in terms of control flows.

In *Object-Oriented Design with Applications* (1991, p.77), Grady Booch then simplifies the definition to the following:

> An *object* has state, behaviour, and identity; the structure and behaviour of similar objects are defined in their common class; the terms instance and object are interchangeable.

He then expands on the meaning and implications of state, behaviour, and identity.

The *HOOD Reference Manual Issue 3.1.1* (p. 2) works from the earlier definition, and states simply:

> An object is a model of a real-world entity, which combines both data and operations working on that data.

This is extended to include abstraction, information hiding and encapsulating principles, thus:

> An object is defined by the services it provides to its users, the services it requires from other objects and its behaviour, whereas the internal structure is hidden to the user, thus giving a view of how it appears to other objects.

However, in order to develop a design, the designer needs more than this, so we will develop a more complete definition of a HOOD object.

3.1.2 Definition of a HOOD object

I suspect that the main reason that people think that finding objects is difficult is that they cannot accept that it is easy, provided that they have a clear understanding of what they are looking for. Bertrand Meyer says that finding objects is 'surprisingly simple', and that 'objects are just there for the picking'. Again, there is a built-in contradiction in many people's minds: that on the one hand there should be a prescriptive or cookbook method for finding objects, while, on the other hand, they would like to stay in employment as software designers with a truly creative role, which would no longer be the case if it were possible to automate the design process completely. Furthermore, there are two forces at opposite ends of the software development life-cycle which are moving to reduce the complexity of this task. Object-oriented analysis (OOA) shifts the emphasis for finding objects into the requirements phase, and ready-to-use libraries of objects or classes provides an infrastructure on which to build in the coding phase. OOA, therefore, will provide the designer with a first set of objects to be used, which will probably be incomplete since it will not include the 'glue' objects needed to make a working design. In addition, the libraries of objects and classes will need to be documented in the design as HOOD objects at some stage to provide a complete design.

How are we to set about finding objects in a wide range of applications? In the term 'application', I include all sorts of program, but in the context of this book, I mean essentially any program that is written in Ada. We must consider a wide scope that includes:

>Embedded systems, where software is built into hardware
>Military or industrial use
>Communication systems
>Workstation-based systems
>Database systems
>Standard data processing systems
>Simulation systems
>Mathematical systems

We need an approach that will not only work well in all environments, but which will also allow for the fact that all features will not be equally significant in all cases. To do this, we need to think about the nature of an object, and how it is used.

The first aspect is based on the object-oriented principle of encapsulation, in which a data item is hidden inside an object and is then accessed or modified through an operation, thus:

An object encapsulates a data item (attribute).

From the perspective of embedded systems, we are also very interested in interfaces to hardware, some of it specially developed for the project, so we should add:

An object may encapsulate a hardware interface and its data.

We have already recognised in the HOOD design process that as well as objects we are looking for operations, and so we can identify the second property of an object:

> An object is an entity that provides operations.

To complete the set, Ada is a strongly typed language, so we include a definition of the type of the data:

> An object provides a type definition of its attributes.

The term 'attribute' is used as a more general term for a data item making up part of the data associated with an object, also reflecting the use of the term in entity relation attribute modelling and in object-oriented analysis. If we consider as an example a bank account, we would expect to have the following attributes and operations associated with it:

Object:	Bank Account
Attributes:	Account Number Customer Reference Balance Credit Limit
Operations:	Open Deposit Withdraw Close Query Balance

The object 'Bank Account' would provide one of the basic components for a banking system, since it could be extended to provide for an interest-bearing deposit account, or a foreign currency account with conversion rate, or a loan account, joint name account, etc.

The next step is to look at the main features in the way we use an object in a software design. It is now time to stress the importance of interfaces. One of the keys to development of a large software project is to have good control of the interfaces between components of software developed by different teams or at different contractors. When these contractors are in different countries, it is easy to see the large impact upon schedules of uncontrolled changes to interfaces, with associated large costs. As the design is made up of a set of interacting objects, each of which provides operations, the next property of an object is:

> An object may require and use the operations provided by other objects.

HOOD, therefore, enables interface control to be based on interfaces between objects, and enables this control to begin early in the design process. The package specification feature of Ada is a great help in providing strong checking of interfaces early in the programming phase, and HOOD brings this forward from the program compilation stage to the architectural design stage, which may be perhaps as much as forty per cent of the software development time, i.e. several months on a long project.

As part of this interface checking, we need to be specific about which objects are interfaced to each other. This is done by defining the scope of visibility. Thus one object *provides* services, and other objects *require* those services. In HOOD terms, this establishes a Use relationship, which corresponds to the Ada context clause used to 'with' another package and provide visibility to the entities in the specification part of the package. We may therefore add that:

> An object has restricted visibility of other objects.

The 'H' of HOOD stands for 'hierarchical'. There are two forms of hierarchy: top-down decomposition hierarchy and seniority hierarchy. The seniority hierarchy results from the partial definition above, and defines the interaction between objects (described in more detail in the next chapter). The decomposition hierarchy, which is developed by the HOOD design process and is reflected in the HOOD design tree, results in the next statement:

> An object may be decomposed into two or more objects which together provide the same functionality.

This statement is crucial to the development of a design of a large, complex software system in which it is necessary to consider the design at a high level of abstraction to arrive at a set of objects which together provide all the functionality of the program, and then to repeat this process on each in turn. Exceptionally, a parent object may be decomposed into a single child object in order to reuse an existing child object while renaming some of its operations, or restricting access to one or more operations in the design.

Having developed an understanding of what an object is and how it behaves, we may return to the question of how we find the objects for an application. Looking at a typical computer program, we see that there is some data input, some processing and some data output. The data input may come from a piece of special hardware, may be seen as operator input, may be a file, communications link or may be a database. Similarly, data output may be directed to special hardware, to an operator display, a file, communications link or database. Any of these real-world 'things' could be mapped into an object since it would certainly require a set of operations to control it, and probably require an associated data item or attribute to be stored in the object.

Object	*Attributes*
Special hardware:	Address
	Status
Operator input:	Buffer
	Status
File:	Name
	Position
	Status (open/closed)
	Error status
Communications link:	Type
	Address
	Speed
	Error count
Database:	Name
	Table name
	Locks
	Buffer

Any of these 'things' represents a real-world entity which should map into an object at the top level of decomposition.

Another general set of sources for objects is the set of data structures of the program, either those defined in the requirements as belonging to the problem, or those defined during the course of design as belonging to the solution. Thus we may have data being read from a device into a buffer; when they are collected into a record, they may be stored in a table, Table_1, and then when they are analysed they may be stored in another table, Table_2, for collation, prior to being interpreted and a result output. Each of these data items, buffer, Table_1, Table_2, may become an object in the design.

Thus to help us to find objects, we have another property of an object:

An object is a model of a real-world entity or a software solution entity.

In order to be able to identify and use an object, the object is given a name, which comes from the analysis of requirements or from the design solution. This name is generally carried into the Ada source code as a package name; it should therefore obey the Ada rules for an identifier:

An identifier starts with a letter, and may be followed by one or more letters or digits, optionally separated by an underline. For example:

    bank_account

This leads to the following statement about an object:

An object is denoted by a name.

In addition, we may identify the following properties of an object which are optional. They are both related to the generalisation of a thing into the set of things of which it is a member. For example, each reader of this book has a name, and is a unique person. He or she is therefore a member of the set of people, and also a member of the set of readers, which is a subset of the set of people. But most of the time we do not go around thinking 'I am a person' or 'I am a reader'. These statements are always true, but are not very important. In the same way, any physical object that we use, from a spoon to a computer, is a member of a class of similar things. We often deal in sets of things, such as a set of cutlery when laying a table, or a set of compatible computers when developing software for the retail market, but in many software systems, especially embedded systems, the concept of class is not all-pervasive. We are often interested in an Ada package to perform a certain set of operations, on a set of data: we may not need a set of similar packages. On the other hand, there are times when we want to have several packages that are similar, for example to handle a set of similar hardware, where we could use Ada generic packages with some parameterisation. In these cases, we may need to think more widely and say that:

An object may be an instance of a class.

HOOD provides a class object to support this statement (see Chapter 5). In terms of developing a definition to help us find objects, though, the concept of class is not so important. This will come later in the design. When we have found a set of objects, we may ask whether each object is better implemented as an instance of a class, either a class that already exists in some library, or a class that should be developed for this project, and with possible reuse in later projects.

Another approach that may be used in developing software is to provide an abstract data type (ADT) package. An ADT also provides a general solution: a package contains a definition of a type as a private type, and also provides the necessary operations for that type, but does not provide a data item on that type. An object of that type may be declared in another package, and then the operations may then be used on that object. A HOOD object may be developed as an ADT, but, in the same way as for a class, the object needs to be identified first, and then implemented as an ADT later. This type of object using an ADT is similar to a C++ class that is defined without any inheritance features. Thus we may say:

An object may be implemented by creating an abstract data type, and then creating an object as an instance of the ADT.

If the requirements have a state transition diagram (STD) or a set of STDs that describe the major states of the program, then the designer should seriously consider having an object to reflect and control the state of the program. This provides a powerful and natural way of expressing the high-level abstraction of control of the design. Such an object may be said to be a 'state machine' if it does not export a type, and so the state is fully encapsulated in the object, accessible and changeable only through the interfacing operations.

Another view is to say that an object that contains data has state implicitly or explicitly. For example, a list has the obvious states of empty and full as well as the normal state of containing some entries. Yet another view is that the actual data content is also part of the state of the object. A list containing the names of three people Tom, Dick and Harry is different from the same list containing the three names John, Paul and Ringo. In either case, we may use an STD to document the design. An object may also be called a state machine if the object fully controls its own state, i.e. the state cannot be controlled from outside the object. Since this is generally true of a HOOD object, we may say:

An object may have state, and may be considered as a state machine, using a state transition diagram to document the design.

This leads to a definition of an object suited to a hierarchical design as follows:

An OBJECT

- encapsulates a data item (attribute)
- provides a type definition of its attributes
- provides operations to other objects
- may require and use operations provided by other objects
- has restricted visibility of other objects
- may be decomposed into two or more objects which provide the same functionality
- is a model of a real-world entity or a software solution entity
- is denoted by a name
- may be an instance of a class
- may be implemented by an abstract data type
- may have state:
  - · may be considered as a state machine
  - · may use a state transition diagram to document the design

From this definition one can see that a system may be composed of a set of objects that provide and require operations of each other. Each object may be a state machine, whose behaviour is described in a state transition diagram, or may be implemented as an abstract data type, or as an instance of a class object, or simply correspond to an Ada package that encapsulates the data on which it works.

A more descriptive definition may be provided as follows:

An object is a model of a real-world entity or a software solution entity that combines data and operations in such a way that data are encapsulated in the object and are accessed through the operations. An object thus provides operations for other objects, and may in turn also require operations of another object. An object may have a state, either explicitly to provide control or implicitly in terms of the value of the internal data. An object may be a class or an instance created as a parameterisation of a class.

3.2 HOW TO FIND OBJECTS: HOOD TEXT APPROACH

In Chapter 2, we described the HOOD Method as consisting of four Basic Design Steps. The first step is to provide a problem definition, which may either consist of references to sections of existing documents, or be a revised description. The second step then sets out to find the top-level HOOD objects by using this information, derived from that provided in the SRD, to establish an informal solution strategy.

From this text, the designer must select the nouns or noun phrases to make a list of objects. This method was conceived by Abbott, and seems at first to be a rather loose and informal approach. But if the designer sees it as a *first* step in identifying candidate objects, which need then to be assessed individually and classified as either object, attribute or value, or discarded as plain noise, then this approach is actually an extension of the statement that:

> An object is a thing

Further selection proceeds according to the properties described in the definition of object above. The selection of nouns or noun phrases may be done by underlining the words in the text. A computer-based tool may use inverse video, boxing, etc., provide automatic underlining of repeats of the selected text, and extract these words to another list for later processing.

The informal solution strategy may be written in normal English, or any other natural language. Alternatively, a project may prescribe a more structured form of English, both as a means to ensure readability and clarity, and to make it easier to analyse the syntax to find objects and operations. A possible formalisation may be defined as follows:

> When <EVENT>   then <ACTION>
> If <CONDITION> then <ACTION>

This type of statement can be analysed as follows:

1. <EVENT> may be an external event, such as a specified time interval, at an interrupt, or when some data arrive. For example:

   > When one second interrupt occurs.

2. <CONDITION> may be when an *object* or an *attribute* of an OBJECT has a defined *state* or *value*, i.e.

   > <CONDITION> ::= <ATTRIBUTE> of <OBJECT> is <STATE>

   For example:
   > If traffic is present.
   > If colour of light is green.

3. <ACTION> may be seen as an operation on an object:

   > <ATTRIBUTE> of <OBJECT> is <OPERATION>ed

   For example:
   > Colour of light is changed to green.

An attribute is, in effect, a data item related to an object, and may in turn become an object if the first object is decomposed. If it is a data item, then a type will be defined for it.

These brief examples identify the *objects* as One Second Interrupt, Traffic, and Light, *value* or *state* as Is_Present, *attribute* as Colour, and *operations* as Occurs, Change_To_Green. Green could also be considered as a *value* of the *attribute* Colour of the *object* Light. Note that some words have been connected with an underscore for two reasons: firstly to combine the words into a definition of the state or operation, and secondly so that a valid Ada-like identifier can be produced.

The names of objects and operations must conform to Ada naming standards and be unique within their scope. Therefore each object name must be unique within a design since an object will map into a package. HOOD requires that each operation name is unique within an object – this is an additional restriction since Ada allows overloading of procedure and function names, providing the parameter lists differ.

If we look at the slightly more complete example of a simple traffic lights system, we can see the pattern of selection. These are the text units that are required.

1.1   Statement of the problem

The traffic lights system controls four traffic lights at a crossroads (roads A, B, C, D), allocating time to each road depending on presence of traffic.

1.2   Analysis and structuring of requirement data

- The system is driven by one second interrupt.
- The main road AC is to be given 40 seconds of green each cycle, and the side roads BD are to be given 20 seconds each cycle if there is traffic waiting for BD, as detected by traffic sensors.
- If there is traffic in only one direction, the lights stay green in that direction.
- If there is no traffic, the main road lights stay green.

2.   Solution strategy

- Initially, set the BD lights red and set the AC lights green.
- When the AC lights are green, count the one second interrupts. After 40 seconds, the BD traffic sensors are checked every second until BD traffic is present, then change the AC lights to amber, then to red. Change the BD lights to red and amber, then to green.
- When the BD lights are green, count the one second interrupts. After 20 seconds, the AC traffic sensors and BD traffic sensors are checked every second until AC traffic is present or BD traffic is not present, then change the BD lights to amber, then to red. Change the AC lights to red and amber, then to green.

To find the objects, we may now analyse the solution strategy by underlining the nouns and noun phrases:

---

2. Solution strategy

- Initially, set the <u>BD lights</u> to <u>red</u> and set the <u>AC lights</u> to <u>green</u>.
- When the <u>AC lights</u> are <u>green</u>, count the <u>one second interrupts</u>. After <u>40 seconds</u>, the <u>BD traffic sensors</u> are checked every <u>second</u> until <u>BD traffic</u> is <u>present</u>, then change the <u>AC lights</u> to <u>amber</u>, then to <u>red</u>. Change the <u>BD lights</u> to <u>red</u> and <u>amber</u>, then to <u>green</u>.
- When the <u>BD lights</u> are <u>green</u>, count the <u>one second interrupts</u>. After <u>20 seconds</u>, the <u>AC traffic sensors</u> and <u>BD traffic sensors</u> are checked every <u>second</u> until <u>AC traffic</u> is <u>present</u> or <u>BD traffic</u> is not <u>present</u>, then change the <u>BD lights</u> to <u>amber</u>, then to <u>red</u>. Change the <u>AC lights</u> to <u>red</u> and <u>amber</u>, then to <u>green</u>.

From this analysis, we may extract the candidate object list as follows:

3.1 Identification of objects

BD lights
red
AC lights
green
one second interrupts
40 seconds
BD traffic sensors
second
BD traffic
present
amber
20 seconds
AC traffic sensors
AC traffic

After this preliminary extraction, we can analyse the list of nouns into objects and other forms as follows:

3.1   Identification of objects

Object	*Description*
seconds	time control of one second interrupt
AC lights	main road lights
BD lights	side road lights
AC traffic sensors	main road traffic sensors
BD traffic sensors	side road traffic sensors

Nouns	*Classification*
red	colour of lights
green	colour of lights
amber	colour of lights
one second interrupts	synonym of seconds
40 seconds	value of seconds
20 seconds	value of seconds
BD traffic	attribute of side road traffic sensors
AC traffic	attribute of main road traffic sensors
present	value of AC/BD traffic attribute

We have now identified five objects, and we may note that **AC lights** and **BD lights** are very similar, so that we have the option of generalising the object in two ways:

1. Create an object **lights** and parameterise the operation **change** with the name of the road pair.
2. Create a class object **lights** and create instance objects for each road pair.

We will leave the class object option until Chapter 5, and continue with the first option, which results in the three objects being:

3.1   Identification of objects

Objects	*Description*
seconds	time control of one second interrupt
lights	lights
traffic sensors	traffic sensors

A similar approach is used to identify the operations. First the verbs in the solution strategy are underlined, and then the verbs are extracted as candidate operations, as follows:

2. Solution strategy

- Initially, <u>set</u> the BD lights red and <u>set</u> the AC lights green.
- When the AC lights are green, <u>count</u> the one second interrupts. After 40 seconds, the BD traffic sensors are <u>checked</u> every second until BD traffic is present, then <u>change</u> the AC lights to amber, then to red. <u>Change</u> the BD lights to red and amber, then to green.
- When the BD lights are green, <u>count</u> the one second interrupts. After 20 seconds, the AC traffic sensors and BD traffic sensors are <u>checked</u> every second until AC traffic is present or BD traffic is not present, then <u>change</u> the BD lights to amber, then to red. <u>Change</u> the AC lights to red and amber, then to green.

3.2 Identification of operations

set	synonym of change
count	
check	
change	

The operations may then be reduced to:

3.2 Identification of operations

count
check
change

These two lists may be combined into the object operation table:

3.3 Object operation table

Object	*Operation*
seconds	count
lights	check
traffic sensors	change

From this table we will be able to derive directly the first draft of the HOOD diagram in Chapter 4.

SOURCES OF OBJECTS

Although this approach of analysing the text into nouns and verbs appears to be rather informal, it can also be successful. It needs to be remembered that it is an approach to aid the designer in finding objects, rather than an automatic prescription, and therefore each candidate object needs to be assessed carefully for suitability for the implementation. One practical approach is for an expert in the system requirements to be invited to describe the requirements to a designer, in which case many of the major objects will be readily apparent in the description. The designer need only note the key words being used, and classify them into objects and operations, to have a good overview of the top-level HOOD design. From this, a continuous and complete design may be developed by reviewing carefully how each of the necessary functions is performed. This interview approach is not a substitute for a good requirements document, but rather complements it by allowing the designer to get an overview of the system before becoming too bogged down in details.

Coad and Yourdon provide the following definition of an object in their book *Object-Oriented Analysis* which may also be helpful in performing the analysis to find objects:

> An object is an encapsulation and an abstraction: an encapsulation of attributes and exclusive services on those attributes an abstraction of the problem space, representing one or more occurrences of something in the problem space.

Another useful background concept is for the designer to understand what may be the source of objects, i.e. where to look to find objects, and the types of object that may be found. There are two major sources: the problem domain and the solution domain.

PROBLEM DOMAIN

Objects may be found in the real world or problem domain, especially at the top level of decomposition. Some OOD methods only have one level of decomposition, in which case this is the main source. It is a strong point about the object-oriented design approach that there is an emphasis on providing a clear mapping from problem to solution, from requirements to design. A major benefit is that it provides good visibility to the person buying the system, either systems designer, operator, or manager, by using the same language at the top level. Many customers are discouraged from reading, reviewing and correcting design documents by the amount of jargon in them and difficulty they have in understanding them. The problem domain sources may be:

1. *Application-dependent*, e.g. radar blip, airplane track, flight number in an air traffic control system.
2. *Hardware devices*, e.g. keyboard, screen, window.

SOLUTION DOMAIN

Objects may also be found in the software or solution domain, in terms of implementation requirements or design solutions. They may be general-purpose mechanisms, such as table, stack, list. An object may be a specific data type for the application, such as a message or command, or an internal message such as transaction control block. An object may be a logical storage device such as a database or file, either required by the problem statement or produced by the design solution.

At the top level of the design, the objects are primarily problem domain objects. At middle levels, there is a mixture of decomposed problem objects and innovative solution domain objects, while at the terminal levels, there may also be reused objects, class instances and a preponderance of software type objects. As the design progresses, different types of object may depend on the design subtree being worked on, so that if a hardware device object is being decomposed, then the child objects would be related to the hardware at a lower level of abstraction.

3.3 OPERATIONS

A similar approach to identifying objects is used to select the verbs in the text and to identify them as candidate operations in the operation identification, and then to assign them to the relevant objects in the object operation table. These operations can then be added to the objects in the HOOD diagram. However, this set may not be complete because it is often necessary to add extra operations to the diagram to complete the communication between objects. In writing the text it is easy to have an implicit access to data, writing something like:

Calculate the altitude from velocity and acceleration

which may need some means of accessing the velocity from a velocity object.

Operations provide access to data and state of an object, and may be of one of three types (Booch/Meyer):

constructor:	changes object state
selector:	evaluates object state
iterator:	visits all parts of the object

These definitions include the idea that *state* includes the data themselves. Thus the state of a list is not only 'empty', 'partially full' or 'full', but also the actual contents. Thus adding an item to a 'partially full' list may leave the list still 'partially full', but there is then an additional item in the list. And the number of entries increase from n to $n+1$.

One may define a list of entries of type card in Ada as a record with the following types and declarations:

```
type state is (empty, partially_full, full);
type card is range 1 . . 13;
type limit is range 1 . . 52;
type cards is array (limit range < >) of card;
type list (max : limit) is
   record
      s              : state;
      entries        : limit;
      card_entries : cards (1 . . max);
   end record;
```

and then two lists may be declared thus:

```
pack : list (52);
hand : list (13);
```

In this example, a constructor would add a card to the list (pack or hand) or delete a card from the list, a selector might ask for the next card or the number of cards in the list, and an iterator might provide each card successively to the user for a user-defined check, e.g. to find the highest card, or a matching suit.

Unfortunately, there are no HOOD rules relating types of operation to object. For example, an object that controls an input device may be said to have only operations of type selector, which read data or status. Another object that controls an output device may have only operations of type constructor that output data, athough the object might also have a selector operation that reads status. However, we can say that an object that contains data without an external input/output interface must have at least one constructor and one selector, so that data are created and then used.

A HOOD tool cannot check the nature of an operation of an object in this way since the tool will not have the intelligence to be able to understand the meaning of the object name or the operation names, and HOOD provides no attribute to identify objects as input or output, nor to classify the operations as constructor, selector or iterator. It is therefore a good idea for a designer to review each object in turn to see whether the set of operations is sufficient, whether data are created but not used, or whether data are used without having been created. This may also be used as a review question for quality assurance.

Overloading is the ability for an operation name to be repeatedly declared/defined within the definition of a single unit, providing that there is some way of differentiating between the definitions, by having different parameters (or arguments). HOOD allows overloading of operations, and, like Ada, also allows an operator to be defined for a new type, and allows an operator to be redefined (overloaded) for an existing type. We look further into the distinction between operation and operator in Chapter 4, section 4.2.

A formal language could be used to specify the requirements or design in the

Operation Control Structure (OPCS) of a critical operation. In this way, a formal language could be applied to those parts of the design that need it and can be specified in this way, limiting the cost of this approach by restricting the scope.

3.4   HOW TO FIND OBJECTS: DATA FLOW DIAGRAM APPROACH

Another approach to finding objects is particularly useful if the requirements are already defined as a set of data flow diagrams (DFDs). In this case, the designer may select candidate objects from the DFD by grouping together either external interfaces or datastores with the corresponding processes and control processes, calling this group a candidate object and adding candidate operations. This approach seems to have a more formal style to it, since the DFD is already a formal statement in diagrammatic form. When the requirements are in another form, it may be useful to draw a top-level DFD to aid in understanding the requirements should you be more familiar with DFDs, and then use this DFD as a basis from which to start.

In the European Fighter Aircraft project, the requirements of some subsystems are collected and documented in great detail in Controlled Requirement Expression (CORE). This resembles a very detailed DFD approach, so either the text or the DFD approach may be followed. In either case, there remains for the designer the important problem of understanding the requirements as a preliminary to performing the design.

Let us look at a very general example first. The simple DFD in Figure 3.1 shows data being read from an input device and stored in a buffer. Data are then read from the buffer and written to the output device. This could be a simple program to copy data from a keyboard onto a screen, or to copy a tape file to a disk file.

In the diagram, input and output devices are represented as external interfaces, also known as source or sink, and shown as named boxes. The buffer is represented as a datastore, and shown as a name between two parallel lines. Each of the operations **read**, **store**, **get** and **write** are shown as process bubbles (ellipse or circle). The dataflow between external interfaces and datastore is shown by an arrow which should be named.

The technique is to select each of the external interfaces and datastores in turn, and add the relevant process bubbles to group them togher as a candidate object, which can then be named. The name of each process bubble can then be added to a candidate object as a candidate operation. Figure 3.2 shows how we may try this on the example DFD.

Figure 3.2 shows three candidate objects called **tape**, **buffer** and **disk**. These names may now be transferred into the 'Identification of objects' section. The operations **read**, **store**, **get** and **write** may be put into the 'Identification of operations' section, and then the two lists may be combined to give the object operation table.

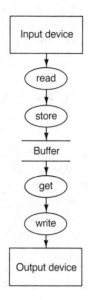

Figure 3.1 Simple data flow diagram.

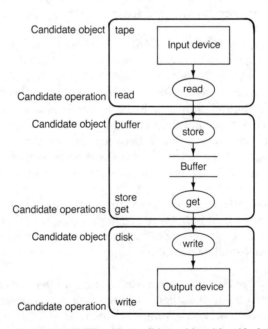

Figure 3.2 DFD with candidate object identified.

3.1 Identification of objects

Objects	*Description*
tape	input device
buffer	data store
disk	output device

3.2 Identification of operations

read
store
get
write

3.3 Object operation table

Object	*Operation*
tape	read
buffer	store
	get
disk	write

A similar approach is illustrated in Figures 3.3 and 3.4 for the traffic light system. Figure 3.3 shows a context diagram, which is the top-level DFD of the program. Here the external interfaces are shown, with a single process bubble to represent the program. The whole diagram has been selected as a single object, which is the top-level object of the design, called **traffic_lights**.

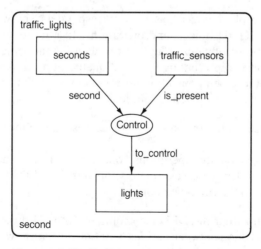

Figure 3.3 Traffic light system – context diagram.

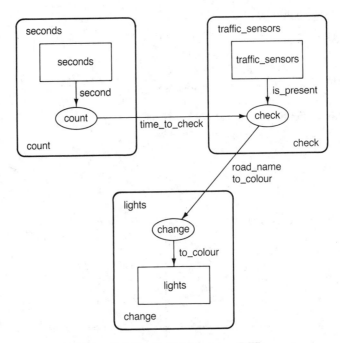

Figure 3.4 Traffic light system – DFD.

In Figure 3.4, further process bubbles have been added to each of the external interfaces and these have been grouped together to form the appropriate candidate objects.

In this simple example, it is easy to see the correspondence between the entities in the DFD and the HOOD objects and operations. In a more complex DFD, this mapping may not be so obvious. The first problem is that some of the processes may be more complex, representing the functionality of more than one operation. This may result in there being only one process between two of the object entities in some cases. There are two possible solutions:

1. Split the process into two or more processes, and allocate each one to a candidate object.
2. Create more candidate operations, one for each candidate object which together constitute the process (i.e. do not alter the DFD but add corresponding operations to the candidate objects).

Another problem is that the DFD may contain a control process bubble, which represents a control action between entities, without any data flow attached. This has two effects:

1. The control flow to the control process may represent an interrupt.
2. The control process may not need any code, but only trigger another process which performs the necessary function.

The natural mapping for a control process is an interrupt. In Ada, an interrupt may be mapped into a representation clause which assigns an address to an entry point to a task, thus:

for <interrupt entry point> use at <address>;

The eventual Ada code will therefore need an entry point, which reflects an operation in the HOOD design. Hence an operation is required for each control process. This operation is called a constrained operation (see Chapter 7, section 7.3).

Let us look at an example of a top-level HOOD diagram derived from a data flow diagram. Figure 3.5 shows a context diagram, and Figure 3.6 the top-level data flow diagram of a simple heating control system. The requirements of the system are defined below:

A simple heating system for a house consists of:

- A start switch and a stop switch to control when the heating system will operate.
- A heater to heat the water.
- A sensor to measure the temperature.
- A required temperature switch to set the required temperature.

Initialisation
When the heating system is switched on, it goes to standby mode.

Standby
When the start switch is pressed, control is enabled.

Control enabled

- The temperature is read from the temperature sensor. The required temperature is read from the required temperature switch.
- If the temperature is less than the required temperature, the heater is switched on.
- When the temperature is more than the required temperature, the heater is switched off.
- When the stop switch is pressed, control is disabled.

Closedown
There is no closedown action.

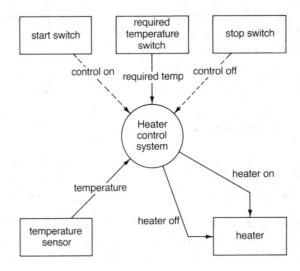

Figure 3.5 Heating control system – context diagram.

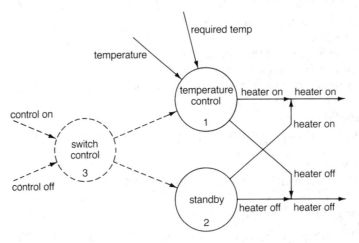

Figure 3.6 Heating control system – data flow diagram.

The main process of the context diagram is called 'heater control system', and is decomposed in the DFD into a control process 'switch control', and two other processes 'temperature control' and 'standby'. The system is started by pressing a start switch and may be switched off by pressing a stop switch.

The process 'heater control system' could have a process specification (P-Spec) that says:

When the start switch is pressed, set control state to enabled (to enable temperature control).
Read the required temperature from the required temperature switch.
Read the temperature from the temperature sensor.
If temperature < required temperature − constant, turn on heater.
If temperature > required temperature + constant, turn off heater.
When the stop switch is pressed, set control state to standby (to wait for start switch).

From the context diagram (Figure 3.5), the following objects may be identified:

start switch
required temperature switch
temperature sensor
heater
stop switch

From the process specification, additional nouns are identified:

temperature	value of temperature sensors
required temperature	value of required temperature switch
control state	object controlling system
constant	smoothing value

Therefore we may add **control state** as an object with an initial operation **start** which is called when the system is first initialised, and we may combine **start switch** and **stop switch** to create a composite object called **switches**. This leads to:

3.3   Object operation table

Object	Operation
control state	start
switches	read start switch
	read stop switch
required temperature switch	read
temperature sensor	read
heater	turn on
	turn off

Figure 3.7 shows the state transition diagram for the system, which is therefore also the STD of the object **control state**.

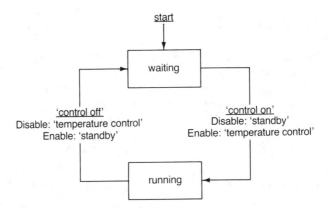

Figure 3.7 Heating control system – state transition diagram.

3.5 CONCLUSION

This chapter has developed a definition of a HOOD object, and described how to find an object. The first approach is the standard HOOD way of analysing the text to find nouns or noun phrases, then classifying the nouns as object, attribute or value, or rejecting the noun as not relevant to the design. The second approach is to analyse a data flow diagram to obtain a set of candidate objects to be classified in the same way. Both approaches lead to an object operation table, which is the basis for the next step of generating a HOOD diagram.

In each case, the relevant documentation in the HOOD Chapter Skeleton format has been shown.

4

HOOD DIAGRAMS

This chapter introduces the most important elements in a HOOD design, and defines the corresponding diagrammatic forms.

4.1 PASSIVE AND ACTIVE OBJECTS
(Ref. *HRM 3.1.1*, section 3)*

HOOD identifies two main types of object according to the control flow within the object. A passive object provides purely sequential control flows, while an active object has its own control flow and may therefore be used to implement concurrency.

4.1.1 Passive objects

Each type of object shares the same basic shape, with a name for the object at the top and a set of names for the operations in a box at the left-hand side. The box represents a definition of the interface of the object, limited to the operations. Other items that are part of the object interface, like types and constants, are not shown in the interface box but are expanded and defined fully in the Object Description Skeleton (see Chapter 6). Figure 4.1 shows the shape of the passive object.

As an example, Figure 4.2 shows an object representing a pump with operations to switch on the pump and to switch off the pump.

* *HRM 3.1.1 = HOOD Reference Manual Issue 3.1.1*

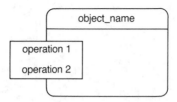

Figure 4.1 Passive object.

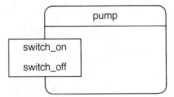

Figure 4.2 Passive object **pump**.

A passive object is mapped into an Ada package, and each operation maps into a procedure or function. The flow of control to each operation is sequential, so that in this example, when the operation **switch on** is called from another object, the procedure or function **switch on** of package **pump** is entered and executed immediately. The flow of control in the calling object is in effect transferred to the called operation **switch on**, and when this completes execution, control is transferred back to the calling operation of the object.

4.1.2 Active objects

The main purpose of an active object is to provide a means of introducing concurrency into a HOOD design. An active object may be defined in two ways, both related to flow of control. The first definition states:

An active object has its own control flow.

This contrasts with a passive object which executes in the control flow of the object which calls one of its operations. In a program consisting solely of passive objects, there is only one control flow and all the operations execute sequentially. In a program with n active objects, there may be $n+1$ interdependent control flows, with one control flow for the program procedure and the passive objects it uses, and a further n control flows for the n active objects.

The second definition is based more closely on the *HOOD Reference Manual* text and states:

> When an operation of an active object is called, control is not necessarily transferred to the operation immediately, but the active object receives an external stimulus. Reaction to the stimulus may be delayed according to the internal state of the object. This constraint is defined in the Object Control Structure (OBCS) of the active object.

The emphasis of this definition is on the control of the interaction between operations of an active object. Thus we see that an Object Control Structure has been introduced to define this interaction. The purpose of the OBCS is to isolate the control aspect into one place, and to define this control early in the design process and at a high level in the program hierarchy.

This important part of the design can be tested in a prototype mode. Of course, when the full program is available, modifications may need to be made to the OBCS if timing problems emerge. The structure of the OBCS is defined in Chapter 6, and the real-time aspects are discussed in Chapter 7. The OBCS is one place to put a timing budget for the active object.

The diagram of an active object is distinguished by a capital 'A' in the top-left corner. A zigzag arrow against one or more of its operations indicates that the operation is constrained according to either the internal state of the object or to the type of execution request. Figure 4.3 shows a general form of an active object.

Figure 4.4 shows the object **pump** modified to be an active object with two

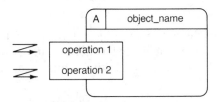

Figure 4.3 Active object.

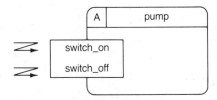

Figure 4.4 Active object **pump**.

constrained operations **switch_on** and **switch_off**. This might, for example, be necessary when there needs to be strict control of the two operations for sensitive equipment, perhaps to allow a time delay between successive invocations of an operation, or to allow an object and its operations to be shared between two other, possibly conflicting active objects.

An active object represents an object with its own flow of control, and as such may carry out its processing independently of other objects, except in as much as there is an interaction or data flow between them. An active object is mapped into an Ada task, and its constrained operations are each mapped into an entry of this task.

There are four ways in which an operation may be constrained:

- If the flow of control to the operation is constrained by the state of the object as represented by the OBCS, then the constraint may be (1) *highly* or (2) *loosely* synchronous.
- If the operation is linked to a hardware or software interrupt, then the operation constraint may be (3) *asynchronous*.
- The operation may have a (4) *timeout* attached or implied.

Constrained operations are described more fully in Chapter 7.

An active object may also have one or more unconstrained operations, which provide access to the data of the object in a synchronous way without any constraint. Exceptionally, and in contradiction to the definition of an object, an active object may also have no operations, in which case it is an actor in the design whose services are not used by any other object. This corresponds to an Ada task that executes after elaboration of the package in which it is defined.

4.2 PASSIVE AND ACTIVE DESIGN

When a program consists solely of passive objects, we may call it a passive design. In this case, we may expect the root object to have one or more operations, as shown in Figure 4.5. There might be an operation **initialise** that is called to set up the initial

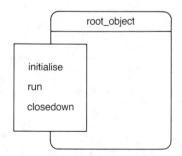

Figure 4.5 Passive design.

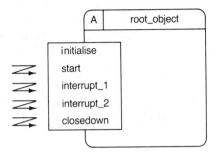

Figure 4.6 Active design.

conditions; an operation **run** to perform the main processing, and an operation **closedown** to provide a controlled closedown of the program. These would be called in sequence from the program main procedure.

One possibility is for the functionality of these operations to be provided by one or more of the objects of the program, in which case there need only be a single operation corresponding to **run**. An embedded system may not need an operation **closedown**, because the program could simply terminate when the computer is switched off.

When a program contains at least one active object, then it is an active design, and the root object is active. Again, there may be an operation **initialise**, which need not be constrained, and an operation **closedown** which might be triggered as a response to an external interrupt to switch off the system gracefully, such as a stop button. In addition, there may be an operation **start** or **run** which may be unconstrained and follow the initialisation, or it may also be constrained to a start button. In addition, every interrupt that the hardware supports should be represented as a constrained operation in the interface of the object. Thus **interrupt_1** and **interrupt_2** are shown in the active design in Figure 4.6.

4.3 OPERATIONS
(Ref. *HRM 3.1.1*, section 3)

The operations of a parent object are defined from the previous stage of decomposition when the object is a child object. For a root object, the parent operations represent the interface to the passive or active design as described in the previous section.

When a parent object is decomposed into child objects, the operations in the object operation table are added to the child objects in the HOOD diagram. HOOD permits an operation to be overloaded so that an operation name may appear more than once in the HOOD diagram. Repeated operations are distinguished in the Provided interface in the Object Description Skeleton.

All operations of a passive object are unconstrained, which means that the operation executes immediately in the control flow of the calling operation. An active object may also have constrained operations, which are defined more fully in Chapter 7, section 7.2. A constrained operation is identified in the HOOD diagram by a trigger arrow, to which may be attached an optional label.

An operation may be mapped into a procedure, a function, or a task entry, or may also be considered as an operator. Each operation name must be a valid Ada identifier for a procedure/function/entry, or represent an operator in the form of a function followed by the operator in quotation marks, thus:

> function "+"

After adding the operations that are listed in the object operation table to the corresponding objects, the designer continues the design process by adding Implemented_By links (see section 4.5) from parent operations to operations of child objects, and Use links (see section 4.6) between objects. As a result of this activity, further operations may be identified and added to the child objects. These additional operations will normally provide access to data encapsulated within an object, rather than provide further functionality. Further refinement of the design of the operations is performed in the Object Description Skeleton (see Chapter 5).

4.4 INCLUDE RELATIONSHIP
(Ref.*HRM 3.1.1*, section 5)

A major part of the HOOD design process is the successive decomposition of objects into child objects. We have seen from the beginning how the system is decomposed into a set of objects. We call the system the root object, because it is the root of the HOOD design tree. This hierarchical decomposition of a parent object into children is called an Include relationship, in which a parent object 'includes' the child objects of which it is composed.

To illustrate the diagram features in this chapter, we will build up a HOOD design for a heating system for a house for which the requirements are given in Appendix D. Figure 4.7 shows the Include relationship in which an object called **heating_system** is decomposed into the objects **timer, pump, heater** and **sensors**. This decomposition process means that all the funtionality of **heating_system** is provided by the set of child objects.

If the parent object is passive, then in general all the child objects will be passive. But a passive object may include an active child object provided that this does not violate the passive properties of the parent (see *HOOD User Manual*, section 5.4). This is discussed further below.

If the parent object is active, then at least one child object must be active, in order to contain the control flow and the constraints between any interacting operations. If there are two or more active child objects, then the active nature of the parent is

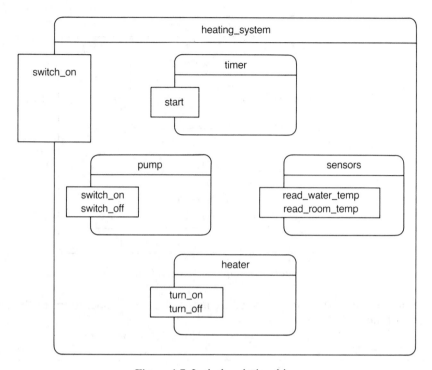

Figure 4.7 Include relationship.

mapped and split between the child objects. This is reflected in the Object Description Skeleton where the Object Control Structure of the parent is implemented by the child objects (see Chapter 5, section 5.6).

4.5 IMPLEMENTED_BY LINK
(Ref. *HRM 3.1.1*, section 5.2.2)

A parent object generally has one or more operations. Since the parent object has to be represented totally by its child objects after the decomposition process, each of these operations has to be mapped into an operation of a child object. This means that when the operation of the parent object is called, then the corresponding operation of a child object is in fact called. This mapping is represented by an Implemented_By link in the diagram, which is a dotted line with an arrow head going from the operation of the parent object to the operation of the child object. Figure 4.8 shows a simple example of the general case, where an object **operator_console** is decomposed into two objects: **keyboard** and **screen**.

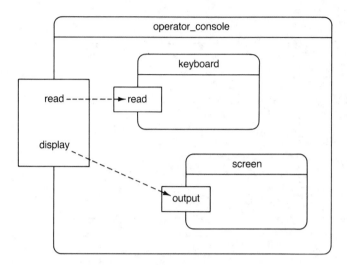

Figure 4.8 Implemented_By link.

The operations of the parent object are mapped onto the operations of the child objects as follows:

operator_console	child object	operation
read	keyboard	read
display	screen	output

This table also shows that the names of the parent and child operations may either be the same (e.g. read) or different (e.g. display/output). Since each name is qualified by the object name, they are always different in global terms.

It is important to remember that this is a one-to-one mapping, so that the parent operation may be thought of as an alias of the child operation. In Ada, it is possible to implement the Implemented_By link as a **rename** of a procedure or function.

Figure 4.9 shows the example diagram extended with an Implemented_By link going from the operation **switch_on** of the parent object **heating_system** to the operation **start** of the child object **timer**. Thus when the operation **switch_on** of object **heating_system** is called, this is automatically replaced by a call to the operation **start** of the object **timer**.

There is one restriction in the Implemented_By link mapping, which is to do with constrained operations. The parent and child operations of an Implemented_By link must both be either constrained or unconstrained. It is not allowed by HOOD

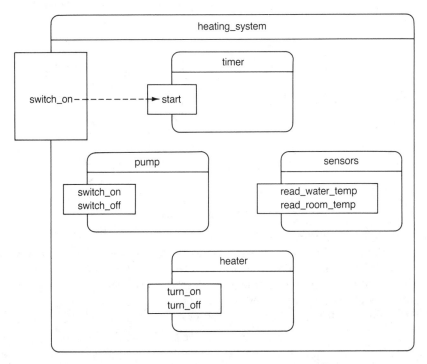

Figure 4.9 Implemented_By link heating system.

rules to map a constrained operation to an unconstrained operation, or vice versa (see *HOOD Reference Manual Issue 3.1.1*, Appendix 4, rules 0–2, 0–3). Thus the constraint is maintained during the decomposition process.

Another aspect of this is that a parent active object with an operation must have at least one active child object, so that each constrained operation of the parent object may be mapped by an Implemented_By link to a constrained operation of a child object. When the parent active object has no constrained operation, then only the active nature, the independent control flow, is mapped into the active child object.

4.6 USE RELATIONSHIP
(Ref. *HRM 3.1.1*, section 4)

We have so far discussed how to break down the program into a set of child objects, and we have ensured that each of these objects has a set of operations that can be used to access or modify data in the object, or to control a hardware interface. In order to turn this into a working program, we need to represent the control flow between the objects. This is done by a Use link between objects. Thus if one object

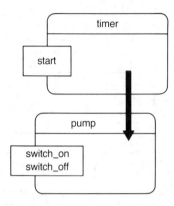

Figure 4.10 Use relationship.

uses an operation of another object, then we draw a Use link between the two objects as a thick arrow from the using object to the used object. This is illustrated in Figure 4.10, which shows an object **timer** that uses an object **pump**, i.e. an operation of object **timer** (in this case operation **start** – the only operation) uses or calls one or more of the operations **switch_on** and **switch_off** of object **pump**.

A definition of a Use relationship is as follows:

> An object is said to use another object if it requires one or more operations of the other object.

A simple way of representing this concept is with the seniority hierarchy shown in Figure 4.11. Each object may use an operation of another object. This Use relationship is identified by an arrow from the using object to the used object. The set of Use links between child objects of a parent define a seniority hierarchy of the objects, similar to an actor–agent–server hierarchy.

In Figure 4.11, the object **actor** uses some of the operations of the objects **agent_1** and **agent_2**, **agent_1** uses some of the operations of the objects **agent_2** and **server**, and **agent_2** uses some of the operations of the object **server**. Thus an **actor** is an object that is not used, an **agent** is an object that is both used and using, and a **server** is an object that does not use another object. This may be represented by the following table:

Object type	Used	Using
actor	–	X
agent	X	X
server	X	–

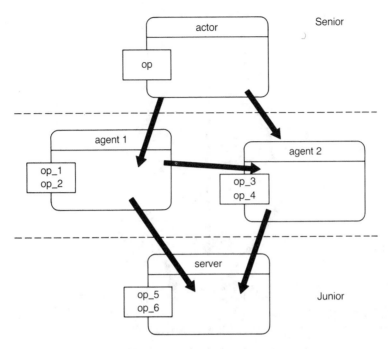

Figure 4.11 Seniority hierarchy.

The concept of seniority hierarchy, or actor–agent–server, is an important part of HOOD, but the dashed lines of Figure 4.11 that divide the objects into layers would not normally appear in a HOOD diagram. However, it is as well to be aware of these concepts, and to structure the HOOD diagram so that this seniority hierarchy is visible, if this is reasonably and topographically possible.

Note also that it is simple and permissible to modify the design by adding a Use link from the object **actor** to the object **server** if it is decided that this is necessary later in the design, so that the object **actor** may use an operation of the object **server**, as in Figure 4.12.

VISIBILITY
It is important to remember that the Use relationship refers only to operations that are provided by the used object: it does not refer to other entities like types, exceptions, constants or data. As a consequence of an object using another object, the using object may need to know about the types associated with the data that are passed as parameters by the used operations. Therefore when the Ada source code is generated, the using object will need to be able to access these definitions by means of a 'with' context clause to the used object.

In this way, a Use relationship implies *visibility* of the object. By visibility, we mean that a using object can see the interface or specification of the used object. So

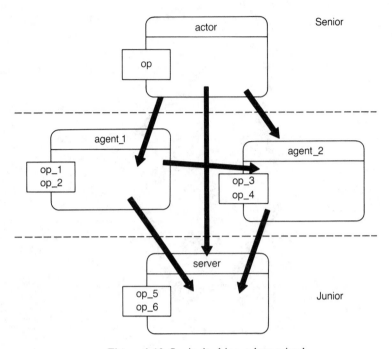

Figure 4.12 Seniority hierarchy revised.

an object may have visibility of another object only if the first object uses an operation of the other object.

In Figure 4.13, the interfaces of objects **pump**, **heater** and **temperature_sensors** are all visible to the object **timer**.

HOOD RULES FOR THE USE RELATIONSHIP
(Ref. *HRM 3.1.1*, Appendix A.2)
There is a set of rules in HOOD, and part of this set relates to the Use relationship. The first rule (U-1) is the definition that we have just seen:

> An object may use another object, i.e. an object requires at least one operation of the used object.

In conjunction with this rule, one may assert that an object may not use itself. This is not to say that an operation of an object may not call another Provided operation of the same object if necessary, but such an activity would not imply a Use relationship, and no Use link would or could be drawn on the HOOD diagram.

The second rule (U-2) is that:

> Passive objects shall not use each other in a cycle.

Figure 4.14 shows that object **timer** uses object **pump**, which in turn uses object

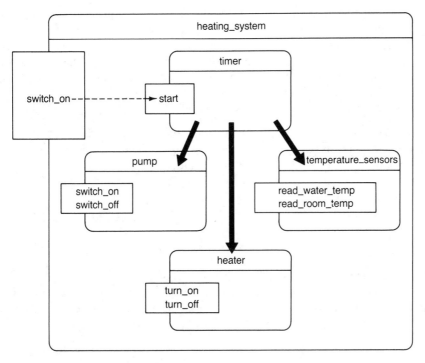

Figure 4.13 Heating system – Use relationship.

tap, which completes the cycle by using object **timer**. This cycle in the Use relationship is not allowed for passive objects.

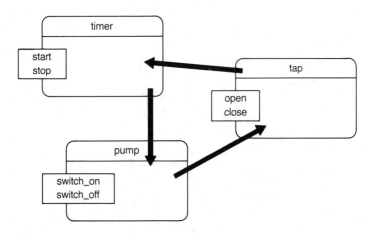

Figure 4.14 Use relationship cycle.

Cyclic Use is allowed for active objects, but is not recommended, since just as cyclic Use relationships between passive objects could lead to recursion, so cyclic Use relationships between active objects could lead to deadlock. If there is a cyclic Use relationship of active objects, then designers and reviewers should look at this carefully to see if the design can be changed to avoid it, and if not, to see what the overall effect is.

The way out of this position of cyclic Use is:

1. It may be that the diagram is in fact wrong, and so it may be modified to form a hierarchy, perhaps by introducing an extra operation to an existing object.
2. To modify the diagram Use links to form a hierarchy.
3. To introduce a new object to control the others, thus making a hierarchy, and a simpler design.
4. To introduce a new object to be used by the others, e.g. providing a buffer or queue.

The main purposes of this rule are:

1. To eliminate the possibility of a loop between objects.
2. To ease testing by ensuring that objects form a hierarchy, so that testing can be done from the bottom up, or, by using stubs, from the top down.
3. To reduce the potential complexity of Use links between objects.

This rule creates, in effect, a hierarchy of objects. The hierarchy should be shown by means of a general direction of flow of the Use arrows from top-left to bottom-right, if reasonably possible. If there is any cyclic Use, then this arrangement will not be possible, and the problem will be clear. There may be some cases where it is more important to show the design structure clearly than to maintain such a flow. An example is shown in Figure 4.15 where data are being read from an input port, sorted and stored into three tables, then processed and sent to an output port.

There are several standard models of Use between objects:

1. One or more independent active objects at the senior level using passive objects at junior levels.
2. Active objects using each other at the senior level in a tree, using passive objects at junior levels.
3. Passive objects in a network.
4. A controlling object, possibly called **state**, which uses the other objects in a simple hierarchy or tree.

The third rule (U-3) is:

A passive object shall not use constrained operations of an active object.

This rule preserves the sequential control flow of the operation of the passive object. It ensures that when an operation of a passive object is used, the operation will execute to completion and return control to the using object without being constrained by the state of any other object.

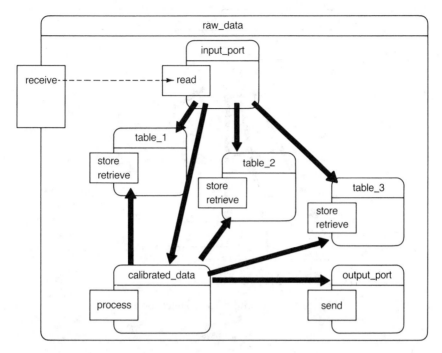

Figure 4.15 Table processing diagram.

The remaining rules require further definitions, and will be introduced with the corresponding definitions.

4.7 UNCLE OBJECT

The Use relationship between two objects is propagated to the children of the using object. Since the children of an object provide all the functionality of the parent object, for each Use relationship of a parent object there must be at least one child object that has the same Use link to any object used by the parent. This may be defined more formally:

> (<A> Uses <B>) and (<A> has child objects) implies there exists a child of <A> that Uses <B>

The corresponding HOOD rule (U-5) states:

> If an object uses another object and has children, then one of its children shall use this object (as an uncle).

Thus the HOOD design tree maps into the HOOD diagram in terms of parent, child and uncle objects.

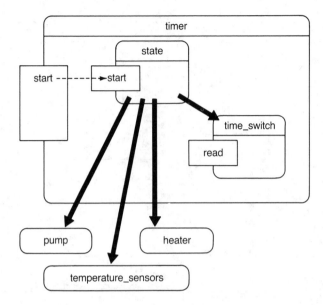

Figure 4.16 Heating system – uncle object.

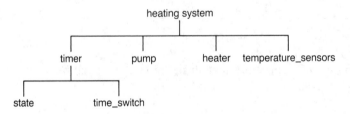

Figure 4.17 Heating system – HOOD design tree.

Returning to the heating system design, let us now decompose the object **timer** into an object **state**, which has state values On and Off, and an object **time_switch**, which is used to read the required periods for the heating system to be on. Figure 4.16 shows the HOOD diagram for object **timer**, with two child objects (**state** and **time_switch**), and three uncle objects (**pump**, **heater** and **temperature_sensors**), each with a Use link from the object **state**. Figure 4.17 shows the corresponding HOOD design tree, which in the nature of a family tree, shows the parent object **timer** at the same level as the uncle objects.

4.8 OPERATION_SET

An operation_set has been provided as shorthand for a set of operations. It is denoted by a name in curly brackets, i.e. {operation_set_name}. In a parent object

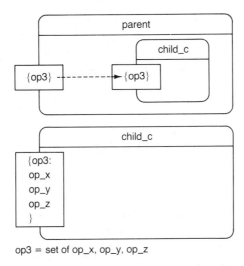

op3 = set of op_x, op_y, op_z

Figure 4.18 Operation_set.

decomposition, the operation_set name must be implemented by an operation_ set of the same name. But this operation_set may be represented at the next lower level by the full set of names of the operations that comprise the operation_set (see *HOOD Reference Manual Issue 3.1.1*, section 5.2.4, and Figure 5.2).

In general, one may expect that the individual operations would be operations of a terminal object, but this is not required. The constituent operation_sets may themselves be decomposed further.

This notation is particularly useful when representing what one may loosely call a pseudo-object such as an operating system – not really an object but it may be useful to describe it in HOOD. In this case, there may be many procedural interfaces to be represented as operations, so there may be operation_sets such as {file_io} and {task_control}.

In Figure 4.18, the operation_set {op3} of the parent object is implemented by the operation_set child_c.op3, which is then decomposed at the level of the child object into three operations called op_x, op_y and op_z. Thus (op3) represents the three operations also at the level of the parent object.

In a similar way, {disk_io} could be used to represent the set of operations {open, read, write, close, seek, check_status} (see Figure 4.19).

4.9 DATA FLOW

A major aspect of an architectural design is to define the data flow. Data can only flow between objects when they are passed as parameters from one operation to another along a control flow, so a data flow is shown in a HOOD diagram by

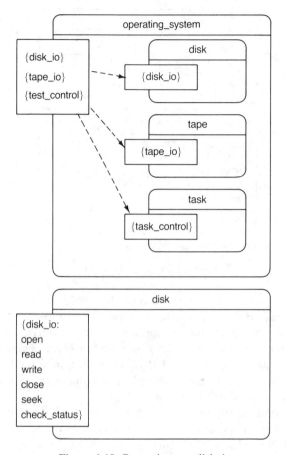

Figure 4.19 Operation_set disk_io.

attaching a named arrow to a Use link. The name may be one or more data items, as a list, and is informal at this point. The flow may be in the same direction as the Use link (In), the opposite direction (Out), or in both directions (In Out). The names and direction of flow are included in the formal description, and represent one or more parameters of the operations used. The direction of flow is mapped into a corresponding Ada mode (In, Out, In Out) for each parameter.

HOOD rule (C-5) states:

> A data flow may exist between two objects only if one object uses the other object through operations with parameters and/or a return value.

This definition allows a data flow to be shown to or from an uncle object. For consistency, a corresponding data flow should be shown at the parent level. Figure

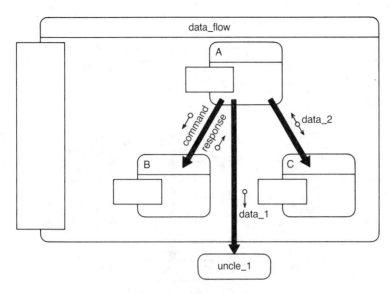

Figure 4.20 Data flow.

4.20 shows data flows in each direction, and also to the uncle object **Uncle_1**. The example in Figure 4.21 (overleaf) shows a data item **temperature** flowing from the object **temperature_sensors** to the object **timer**, although the Use link, which represents the control flow, is in the opposite direction from **timer** to **temperature_sensors**.

Since only major data flows need to be shown in a HOOD diagram, a data flow is informal, and there is no clear and formal mapping from a data flow to the parameters of the operations. This is a weakness compared with other structured design methods, such as data flow diagrams. The result is that in order fully to understand the data flows, the designer should prepare a Cross-Reference Report of Data Flows versus Operation Parameters. Such a report can be produced and maintained by a CASE tool.

4.10 EXCEPTION FLOW
(Ref. *HRM 3.1.1*, section 7)

The Ada language has a concept called an *exception* (*Ada Language Reference Manual*, 11), which is a facility for dealing with errors or other exceptional conditions that arise during program execution. The main principle is that when a subprogram finds an unusual situation, it raises a named exception, which is then processed in another part of the program called an exception handler. HOOD provides for the transfer, or *propagation* of exceptions from one object to another, when one object uses the other. This is intended as an architectural design feature, and is shown in a

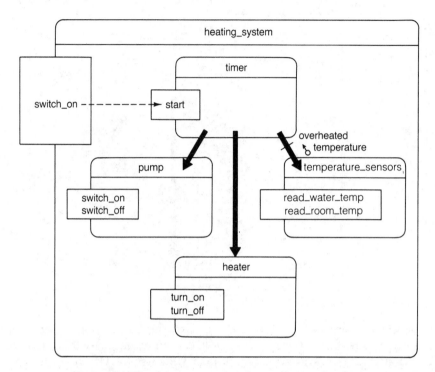

Figure 4.21 Heating system – data flow and exception flow.

HOOD diagram as a named bar across a Use link. The exception is raised by an operation of the used object, and is handled by an exception handler of an operation of the using object. The direction of flow of an exception is thus opposite to that of the Use link.

It is clear that in order for an exception to be propagated from one object to another, there must first have been a procedure call from an operation of one object to an operation of the other object, which gives rise to the HOOD rule (U-6) which states that:

> An exception can only be raised between two objects if one object uses another.

Figure 4.22 shows a general example where an exception called **exception_name** is raised by either **op_1** or **op_2** of object **raising_object**, and is handled by an exception handler in either **op_a** or **op_b**, or both, of object **using_object**.

An exception flow **overheated** is also shown in Figure 4.21 as a bar on the Use link between objects **timer** and **temperature_sensors**, which implies that one or both of the operations **read_water_temp** and **read_room_temp** raises the exception **overheated**, and that an operation of object **timer** handles the exception – it may be operation **start** or an internal operation of the object or an operation of a child of **timer** that actually calls the operation **temperature_sensors.read_water_temp**.

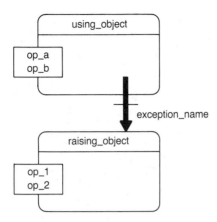

Figure 4.22 Exception flow.

In order to look at the possibilities a little further, let us consider a fragment of HOOD diagram for a pumping system (Figure 4.23) with a timer, pump and a level checking mechanism. The object **timer** is started and switches on the pump via **pump.switch_on**, which then checks the level until the tank is full. The operation **level.check** then raises an exception **full** to inform the object **pump** that the tank is full, and control returns to the object **pump**. The object **pump** may then handle the exception, perhaps by calling its other operation **switch_off**.

If the object **pump** does not have an exception handler for the exception **full**, then the exception is automatically propagated to the object **timer**, which may then provide an exception handler to call operation **pump.switch_off** to switch off the pump.

Alternatively, object **pump** may handle the exception **full**, and raise another exception **full**, which object **timer** would handle as coming from **pump** and being called **pump.full** instead of **level.full**. Thus HOOD provides a design feature to show exceptions on a Use link between two objects, with the possibility for further propagation following Ada rules.

While HOOD specifically supports an exception along a single Use link only, which is not as extensive as the full Ada exception handling system, there is no restriction in using exceptions in the design in other ways. Exceptions may be raised in the Ada source code, and handled wherever required. There may also be exception handlers for all predefined Ada exceptions without these being shown in the HOOD diagram. The feature for unhandled exceptions 'when others' may be put in the Ada source code when required.

It is also worth noting that an exception is not *propagated* along an Implemented_ By link, which represents an equivalence of two operations. However, if an exception is raised by a child object, and is not handled by another child object, then it will, by default, eventually be propagated from a child operation to a parent operation, and then to the object using the parent object.

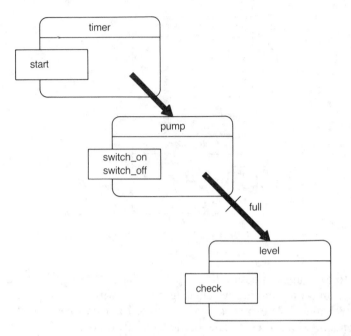

Figure 4.23 Exception flow – pumping diagram.

In the generalised example in Figure 4.24, A.op1 calls B.op2, which is implemented by C.op3, which in turn calls D.op4. Let us suppose that D.op4 raises an exception D.X, which is propagated to object C. Operation C.op3 should then handle the exception, and C.op3 may, if necessary, raise another exception C.Y to be propagated along the Use link to object A. If, however, C.op3 does not handle exception D.X, then D.X will, by default of the Ada exception system, be propagated to object A automatically. Note that this would represent a failure by the designer to provide specific exception handling for the exception raised. Note also that when the exception raised in object B is to be handled in object A, a better design is to introduce another exception. B.Y, raised by object B, which is in turn implemented by an exception C.Y, raised by object C, rather than to allow the exception X raised in object D, which is called D.X, to be propagated to an uncle object.

4.11 ENVIRONMENT OBJECT
(Ref. *HRM 3.1.1*, section 8)

Early users of HOOD found that they needed to be able to describe interfaces to objects or software outside the program that was being designed. The HOOD design

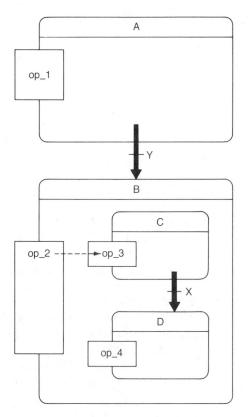

Figure 4.24 Exception propagation.

tree represents primarily the design of an Ada program. But this program may incorporate either one or more existing Ada packages, or it may require objects or packages to be designed by another team or contractor. HOOD provides the environment object to represent such a package or object in the design, so that the external interfaces of the object may be checked as part of the design process, as early as possible, instead of leaving this checking to the compilation stage.

Thus an environment object is not part of the program being designed, but provides a definition of the context or environment in which the design is to be used.

The *HOOD Reference Manual Issue 3.1.1* has taken this general concept a little further than previous issues by stating that: 'An environment object is a *view* of a root object which is not part of the current HOOD design tree but whch is used by the program being designed.' Whereas in earlier issues of the manual, an environment object had only a Provided interface, which was sufficient to allow the external interfaces to be validated, in *Issue 3.1.1* an environment object is a full root object in the HOOD design tree. Of course, only the Provided interface of the Object Description Skeleton needs to be completed to allow interface checking. An

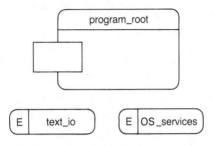

Figure 4.25 Environment object.

environment object is represented as an uncle object in a HOOD diagram, with an additional letter 'E' at the left as the object type letter.

In Figure 4.25, two environment objects are shown to represent existing objects: **text_io** is the standard Ada package and **OS_services** is the environment object representing the operating system services.

If a HOOD design uses an environment object, that environment object need appear in a HOOD diagram only where it is used. It may also appear at other, higher levels if the designer wishes. Consequently, a design that uses many environment objects is not overburdened with environment objects in the higher-level diagrams. This supports the important principle to provide all necessary information to the designer without giving so much that it is confusing (abstraction). The HOOD diagram therefore gives the design detail at a particular level, and the system configuration and HOOD design tree give the overall picture, including all environment objects.

5

OBJECT DESCRIPTION SKELETON

5.1 OBJECT DESCRIPTION SKELETON STRUCTURE

The Object Description Skeleton (ODS) is a structured text format that is used to provide the transition from the formal but incomplete diagram to the Ada source code. The ODS is like a PDL (Program Definition Language), and has a formal layout which can be checked for completeness and consistency. An initial version of the ODS can also be generated from the diagram by a HOOD toolset, and can be updated automatically whenever certain relevant changes are made. Thus a HOOD toolset can normally maintain consistency between diagrams, ODS and Ada code throughout the software engineering life-cycle.

The ODS starts with all the design data that have been put into the HOOD diagram, and is then refined by the designer to include a more explicit definition of the interfaces (i.e. the operations, the parameters of the operations), and of the internal design of the object. The HOOD diagram contains the following design data for each parent object:

Object name
Object type
Provided operations, operation sets and exceptions
Constrained operations for an active object
Used objects, i.e. uncle objects and environment objects
Child objects
Implemented_By links for operations and operation_sets from a parent object
to a child object

Dataflows between child and uncle objects
Exception flow between child and uncle objects

All of this information is common to the diagram and to the ODS. The purpose of the ODS is, therefore, to refine these data further in term of the parameters of the operations, the types, data and constant declarations, operation-to-operation mapping, adding new internal operations and defining the internal logic of each operation.

Since the ODS has a formal structure, it can be analysed and checked by a HOOD tool. The most important check is on the interfaces between objects, ensuring that when one object requires certain services from another object, then the second object does provide those services in its interface. In addition, an editor for the ODS can ensure that the correct syntax for each Ada entity is followed when it is entered by the designer.

The ODS contains seven main sections:

1. The object definition.
2. The Provided interface.
3. The Object Control Structure (OBCS).
4. The Required interface.
5. Data and exception flows.
6. The Internals.
7. An Operation Control Structure (OPCS) for each operation.

Each of these sections is contained within an overall object envelope, which can be represented as shown opposite.

It should be pointed out that the ODS definition given in the *HOOD Reference Manual Issue 3.0* is different in format from the ODS in *Issue 3.1.1* which is described here. However, it is very similar in concept, though lacking some of the features of the ODS of *Issue 3.1.1*. Users of a HOOD toolset that is based on *Issue 3.0* may therefore use this chapter as a tutorial, making allowance for minor variations of layout.

In the examples of the ODS in this and other chapters, the detailed syntax of each field is taken from *HOOD Reference Manual Issue 3.1.1*, Appendix C, 'Backus Naur Form of the ODS'. Particular points to note are:

1. Under each heading of the ODS, information is entered in a list as a declaration or definition. Each entry (e.g. each declaration or object) in a list is separated by a semi-colon.
2. The set of entries in the headings in the PROVIDED_INTERFACE, REQUIRED_INTERFACE FORMAL_PARAMETERS, REQUIRED_ INTERFACE items, and INTERNALS may be given in any order, since some definitions and declarations may need to be in a certain order for successful Ada compilation. For example, a type declaration may require a constant to define an array size, or a data definition may be initialised by a function call.

OBJECT DESCRIPTION SKELETON

OBJECT Object_name IS Object_type
[Class_formal parameters]
[PRAGMA TARGET_LANGUAGE language]

DESCRIPTION
object_description_text

IMPLEMENTATION_OR SYNCHRONISATION_CONSTRAINTS
implementation_constraints_text

PROVIDED_INTERFACE
provided_interface_definitions

OBJECT_CONTROL_STRUCTURE
obcs_synchronisation

REQUIRED_INTERFACE
required_interface_definitions

DATAFLOWS
dataflow_definitions

EXCEPTION_FLOWS
exception_flow_definitions

INTERNALS
internal_definitions

OBJECT_CONTROL_STRUCTURE
obcs_implementation

OPERATION_CONTROL_STRUCTURES
operation_definitions

END_OBJECT Object_name

3. A free text description or annotation may be added after each declaration or definition, but is given sparingly in the examples to avoid confusion. Each text annotation is delimited by --| and |--.
4. When a list is empty, the keyword NONE may be used. In the human readable form (e.g. for a document printout or a screen display), an empty section may be omitted completely. When a group of sections is empty, the whole group may be omitted. This is to reduce the amount of null information that is presented to the human reader, but a computerised HOOD tool needs to store a suitable, modifiable structure.

5. A parameter of an operation may have a default value in the Ada format of:

   parameter : mode type := default_value;

   For example:

   number_of_days : IN integer := 0;

6. An Object Control Structure (OBCS) occurs only in an active object.
7. An Operation Control Structure (OPCS) occurs only in a terminal object.
8. When an object does not use another object, e.g. the root object or a server object, then the Required interface may be NONE.
9. If there are inconsistencies between the BNF of the ODS and the description of the ODS in the main body of the text of the *HOOD Reference Manual Issue 3.1.1*, then the BNF in Appendix C is the authorised version.

5.2 OBJECT DEFINITION

```
OBJECT Object_name IS Object_type
   [Class_formal_parameters]
   [PRAGMA TARGET_LANGUAGE language]

DESCRIPTION
   object_description_text

IMPLEMENTATION_OR_SYNCHRONISATION_CONSTRAINTS
   implementation_constraints_text
```

HEADING
The first section is the basic information about the object. The object_name and object_type are obtained directly from the HOOD diagram. The object_type may be one of:

PASSIVE
ACTIVE
ENVIRONMENT PASSIVE
ENVIRONMENT ACTIVE
CLASS PASSIVE
CLASS ACTIVE
INSTANCE_OF
OP_CONTROL
VIRTUAL_NODE

The object_type affects the layout of the ODS since certain parts of the ODS are optional. In addition to the fields above, the following optional sections are included according to object_type:

PASSIVE	no OBCS
ACTIVE	contains OBCS
ENVIRONMENT	PROVIDED_INTERFACE only
CLASS	contains FORMAL_PARAMETERS
INSTANCE_OF	refers to CLASS and has PARAMETERS
	no OBCS or OPCS
OP_CONTROL	no PROVIDED_INTERFACE
	INTERNALS contain one OPCS
VIRTUAL_NODE	allocation to physical node
	always a parent so no OPCS

Environment, class and instance objects are described in Chapter 4, and the variations in the ODS for each of these object types is given later in this chapter. The Op_Control object is fully described with its ODS in Chapter 7, and the virtual node object is described in Chapter 9.

DESCRIPTION

The description field contains an object description text which is a natural language description of what the object does. This description corresponds to, and should be copied from, the HOOD Informal Solution Strategy detailed in Chapter 2, section 2.2.2.

CONSTRAINTS

The object description is supplemented by a description of the dynamic aspects of the object in a field called IMPLEMENTATION_OR_SYNCHRONISATION_CON-STRAINTS (or the shorter form IMPLEMENTATION_CONSTRAINTS), which contains the synchronisation, control sequence or other special design require-ments. This part applies specifically to active objects and virtual node objects. These constraints will later be detailed and formalised in the Object Control Structure (OBCS) described below. Such things as connection to hardware in-terrupts, timer control and prevention of deadlock mechanisms should be included here.

5.3 PROVIDED INTERFACE

The Provided interface section contains a formal description of the resources provided by this object to any other object that uses it. These will all appear in the Specification of the Ada implementation.

If the object is a parent object, each item in the Provided interface may be implemented by an equivalent item in a child object Provided interface. The Implemented_By mapping or the actual definition of the item is given in the Internals section of the ODS.

PROVIDED_INTERFACE
-- provided_interface_definitions

TYPES
    List of Types with Definition and Description

CONSTANTS
    List of Constants with Description

OPERATION_SETS
    List of Operation_sets with Description

OPERATIONS
    List of Operations with Parameter list, optional Return Type,
    operation_set membership and Description

EXCEPTIONS
    List of Exceptions with Raising operations & Description

TYPES

The first section contains the types that the object provides. For each type, the ODS will contain the type name followed by a description of the type. In addition, there may be a full definition of the type in Ada syntax. These type names are therefore visible to all other objects that use this object, which are either child objects of the same parent or uncle objects. The types are also visible to the parent object Internals, for example for declaration of a data item. Provided types are not visible to the object's own child objects, but are each implemented by a Provided type of a child object, which in turn is visible to the child object or a using object.

For a terminal object, the types that are defined here are essentially the types of the data that are encapsulated in the object, i.e. the types of the object itself.

For a parent object, a type may be implemented by a type of a child object, this relationship being defined in the ODS Internals (see section 5.7.2).

A type may be any Ada type except a task type. Thus a subtype, a derived type, or a record type is allowed here. A private type, a limited private type or an incomplete type will need to be completely defined in the Internals.

If the type of the object is a record, then the component types of the record may be defined at the parent level or may be defined at a lower-level child object which properly owns the type, in which case a construct like the following is required:

```
      type parent_type is private;
  private
      type parent_type is
        record
            value : child.child_type;
        end record;
```

Note that a parent that is implemented by a type of a child object will be mapped into an Ada subtype as follows:

TYPES
    parent_type IMPLEMENTED_BY child.child_type

will map into the Ada:

    subtype parent_type is child.child_type;

Use of types in a HOOD design is discussed more fully in Chapter 8, section 8.3.

CONSTANTS

Constants that are needed by other objects are listed next with a description, and are declared in the Internals.

OPERATION_SETS

The operation_set names from the HOOD diagram are listed with a textual description. The Implemented_By mapping is defined in the Internals.

OPERATIONS

The next item that the object provides are the operations, which correspond directly to the operations identified in the HOOD Chapter Skeleton 3.3 and in the diagram. The parameters are added to the extent that these are known at this stage of the design. The data already identified by the data flow icons should be put in immediately, using the mode IN, IN OUT or OUT according to the direction of the dataflow icon arrow head. As the objects and operations in the design are further refined, it will become more apparent what the necessary parameters are.

An unconstrained operation may have a return type, so that it will then be mapped into an Ada function.

An operation may be defined to be a member of an operation_set that is already defined in the Provided interface above. This is the point at which an operation_set is itself split into operations.

The full syntax for each entry in this section is:

    operation_name [(list of parameter : [mode] type)]
    [RETURN type] [MEMBER_OF operation_set_name] [text annotation];

An example is:

    read_sensor (sensor_address : IN address) RETURN present
    MEMBER_OF commands; --| read a single sensor |--

EXCEPTIONS

Lastly, any exceptions identified by the exception flow icon in the HOOD diagram should be included. These are the exceptions that are raised by the operations of this object to any other object that uses this object. An exception is a design technique that provides a mechanism for passing control back to the using object in an unusual or error condition: it provides an alternative to having an error code as a parameter, and has the advantage that the processing is more efficient in the normal case. However, exceptions are not provided by many languages other than Ada, and so its use should be restricted to designs for which the language provides a suitable facility. (The latest version of C++ has a powerful exception feature which allows one function to *throw* an object in order to transfer control to a handler which may then *catch* the object and take appropriate action according to the contents of the object. The object may be anything, such as a string, a data variable or a complex data structure of a C++ class or struct.)

In general, the Provided interface will always include operations, since this is the main criterion for a good object, i.e. that it encapsulates data with the operations that are needed on the data, and without operations the object cannot be executed. One special case is for an object which represents a package that only provides types, such as an environment package. (This is an implementation method to allow the whole program knowledge of the data structures being manipulated; it does not infringe upon the data-hiding principles since no data are contained in them, only how the data are represented. Another case is an active object that need not have any operations since it will execute when it is elaborated as an Ada task.)

The Provided interface may often include types, since types provide visibility into the structure of the data which are internal to the object, and which are provided to the other objects by the parameters to the operations.

5.4 REQUIRED INTERFACE

The Required interface defines the services of other objects that are to be used by this object.

REQUIRED INTERFACE
-- required_interface_definitions

-- for child objects of a Class Object:

FORMAL_PARAMETERS
  TYPES
    List of Types

  CONSTANTS
    List of Constants

  OPERATION_SETS
    List of Operation_Sets

  OPERATIONS
    List of Operations, optionally with Parameter list

  -- for each Required Object:

OBJECT Object_name

  TYPES
    List of Types

  CONSTANTS
    List of Constants

  OPERATION_SETS
    List of Operation_Sets

  OPERATIONS
    List of Operations, optionally with Parameter list

  EXCEPTIONS
    List of Exceptions to be handled

FORMAL PARAMETERS

When the object is a child object of a class object, the first part of the Required interface is a definition of the formal parameters of the class object that are needed by this object. For example, a type **position** may be a formal parameter of a class object, and this type may be needed by a child object of the class object as part of the decomposition of the class object.

Note that operation_set should not be used as it is not easily mapped into Ada (see Chapter 6, section 6.2).

OBJECTS
The second part of the Required interface is a definition of all those services that are
required by the OBCS or OPCS of this object, i.e. the union of all required parts of
the Provided interfaces of all other objects that are used by this object. First the name
of each used object that has been identified by a Use link in the HOOD diagram is
given. This is followed by the relevant required types, constants and exceptions, and
at least one operation or operation_set.

The name of each used or required object is listed. For each object, the following
set of fields is provided:

TYPES
    The names of used types are listed.
CONSTANTS
    The names of used constants are listed.
OPERATION_SETS
    The names of used operation_sets are listed.
OPERATIONS
    The names of used operations are listed. A parameter list may be given in
    order to distinguish between multiple overloaded operation names provided
    by the same object.
EXCEPTIONS
    The names of exceptions raised by used objects that are to be handled by this
    object are listed.

5.5 DATA AND EXCEPTION FLOWS

DATAFLOWS
    List of (Data_Name Direction Object_Name)

EXCEPTION FLOWS
    List of (Exception_Name <= Used_Object_Name)

The data names from the diagram are listed with the corresponding flow direction to another used object, shown by an arrow made up of the equal sign '='
and a comparison operator '<' or '>', i.e. the direction may have the following
values:

Mode	Direction
IN	=>
IN OUT	<=>
OUT	<=

For instance, to represent a data flow of the data name **to_colour** from the object
seconds to the object **lights**, the object **seconds** would have the data flow:

to colour => lights

Exception flows are shown in a similar way, but the direction of flow is always from the used object to the using object, from the server to the actor. Thus to represent an exception **Bus_Error** being raised by object **IO_Bus** and handled by the object **Local_Area_Network**, the object **Local_Area_Network** would have the lines:

> EXCEPTION FLOWS
> Bus_Error <= IO_Bus

Note that this corresponds to an entry in the Required interface of this object under the heading of the object **IO_Bus** with a Required exception **Bus_error**, thus:

> REQUIRED_INTERFACE
> OBJECT IO_Bus
>
>   . . .
>
> EXCEPTIONS
> Bus_Error

5.6 OBJECT CONTROL STRUCTURE

OBJECT_CONTROL_STRUCTURE -- obcs_synchronisation

DESCRIPTION
   text
 	
CONSTRAINED_OPERATIONS
   List of Operations [CONSTRAINED_BY Label]

OBJECT_CONTROL_STRUCTURE -- obcs_implementation

PSEUDO_CODE
   Pseudocode description of Object behaviour
 	
CODE
   Source code in target language
 	
IMPLEMENTED_BY
   List of Active Child Objects

The Object Control Structure (OBCS) is defined for each active object. It appears in two parts. The first part of the OBCS is in the interface or visible part of the object and contains the description and the list of constrained operations. The second part of the OBCS is in the Internals, and consists of a definition in pseudocode and then in Ada source of the interrelationship between the constrained operations of the object, in terms of Ada rendezvous semantics.

DESCRIPTION

The first item is a description of the real-time constraints in natural language. It might include such phrases as:

> 'Entry X is entered every 10 milliseconds'
> 'Entry Y is attached to hardware interrupt 4 which signals receipt of a character from the telecommand equipment'

CONSTRAINED_OPERATIONS

The second item is a list of constrained operations, which are those operations that are marked by a trigger in the HOOD diagram. There may also be an optional label attached to the trigger. This label may be of the following types:

> Highly synchronous execution request (HSER)
> Loosely synchronous execution request (LSER)
> Asynchronous execution request (ASER)
> Timed out execution request (TOER)

(These labels are treated in Chapter 7.) For example, an operation that is activated by an external interrupt at a specified address is specified here by:

> <operation> CONSTRAINED_BY ASER_by_IT<interrupt_address>

So, an operation attached to interrupt at address 101 is given by:

> equipment.start CONSTRAINED_BY ASER_by_IT101

This may be considered as a design statement, or it may be used to generate the necessary source code in the required target language. For Ada, a representation clause attaching the entry point for the operation to the interrupt address is required. Other languages may require some assembler code to handle the interrupt.

PSEUDO_CODE

The next item of the OBCS is the pseudocode. This comprises a definition (in Ada rendezvous semantics or in another formal notation) of the interaction between each operation, i.e. each Ada task entry point. This pseudocode should be close to the final Ada code for the real-time rendezvous aspect of the object. This is important because the emphasis of the early part of the design is on interfaces and on inter- actions between them. Of these, the most critical is the rendezvous. Consequently, after this stage of the architectural design has been completed and tested at the top prototype level, the rest of the design should be more sequential. The most difficult part will have been done, subject to further revision during testing of the full system.

CODE

The pseudocode is implemented as Ada source code, which will be embedded by the Ada code generator as the control part of the Ada task that will be generated for the active object.

IMPLEMENTED_BY

When an active object is a parent object and is decomposed into child objects, the OBCS of the parent object will be implemented by the OBCS of one or more child objects. This design fact is recorded in the IMPLEMENTED_BY section instead of having PSEUDO_CODE and CODE sections.

It is worth noting that a typical design will have a small number of terminal active objects, and therefore the OBCS exists in detail in only these few objects.

5.7 INTERNALS

```
INTERNALS
  -- internal_definitions

OBJECTS
  NONE | List of Child Objects

  TYPES
  List of Provided Type IMPLEMENTED_BY Object.Type
  List of Provided Type Declaration
  List of Internal Type Declaration

CONSTANTS
  List of Provided Constant IMPLEMENTED_BY Object.Constant
  List of Provided Constant Declaration
  List of Internal Constant Declaration

OPERATION_SETS
  List of Operation_Sets IMPLEMENTED_BY Object.Operation_Set

OPERATIONS
  List of Provided Operation IMPLEMENTED_BY Object.Operation
  List of Provided Operation IMPLEMENTED_BY Op_Control_Name
  List of Internal Operation Declaration

EXCEPTIONS
  List of Provided Exception IMPLEMENTED_BY Object.Exception

DATA
  List of Data Declaration
```

Having described the interfaces to the object, both those provided by the object, corresponding to its specification in Ada terms, and those required by the object and therefore to be provided by other objects, we move onto the definition of the Internals of the object. This part of the ODS of the object corresponds to the body of the package in Ada terms. Whereas the Provided interface and Required interface can be defined as soon as the object itself is identified, some of the Internals can only be defined when the object has been decomposed into its component child objects. Of course, some objects will be at the bottom level of decomposition and therefore will not have entries in some fields, and some design data will not become apparent until further levels of decomposition: so one should not expect that all this information can be provided in one design step.

The order of the subsections of the Internals is the OBJECTS subsection first, followed by the other subsections in any order, repeated where necessary, to permit simple generation of Ada source code while allowing for necessary dependencies between entries, as for the Provided interface.

OBJECTS

The first item is a list of the child objects internal to the object. This requires the object to have been considered as a parent, and to have been decomposed into child objects.

TYPES

An important part of the design process is the definition of the relevant types and data for each object. Whereas data should generally be encapsulated in lower-level, terminal objects, accompanied by the type definitions, the corresponding types may also need to be visible across a wider range of objects. This is supported by the option of Implemented_By types from parent object to child object as part of the decomposition process.

Thus a parent object will have statements of the form:

Provided Type IMPLEMENTED_BY Object.Type

for each of those types which are not defined in the Provided interface, and which map the parent Provided type onto a child object Provided type, by means of a subtype (*HOOD Reference Manual Issue 3.1.1*, section 14.2.2, AG-5). For example:

TYPES
    monitor_limit IMPLEMENTED_BY sensor.reading_type;
      --| ensure that limit is same type as reading |--

A terminal object will have a definition for each type in the Provided interface and for each type in the Internals. For example:

TYPES
    reading_type is range 0..255; --| 8-bit register |--

CONSTANTS

For each constant in its Provided interface, a parent object will have a statement of the form:

Provided Constant IMPLEMENTED_BY Object.Constant

which maps the constant onto a constant in the Provided interface of a child object. For example:

CONSTANTS
upper_limit IMPLEMENTED_BY sensor.max_limit;

A terminal object will have a full constant declaration for each constant in its Provided interface, as well as additional Internal constants, in the form:

Provided Constant Declaration
Internal Constant Declaration

For example:

CONSTANTS
max_limit : integer := 240; --| actual upper limit of sensor |--

Internal constants are visible only to the OBCS and OPCS of the object itself.

OPERATION_SETS

For a parent object, the Implemented_By link mapping in the HOOD diagram is repeated in the ODS in text form here for each operation_set in the Provided interface.

OPERATIONS

For a parent object, each operation in the Provided interface is mapped onto either a child object Provided operation or onto an Op_Control object as follows:

Provided Operation IMPLEMENTED_BY Object.Operation
Provided Operation IMPLEMENTED_BY Op_Control_Name

Op_Control objects are described in Chapter 7.

For a terminal object, the ODS may declare further operations as follows:

Internal Operation Declaration

Internal operations do not appear in the HOOD diagram; they are visible to the OBCS and to the OPCS of other operations. Internal operations allow scope for decomposing a complex or large Provided operation into a hierarchy of Internal operations, or for implementing a common operation for more than one Provided operation as part of the lower levels of design of an object. For example, low-level I/O may be handled by an Internal operation, and may be used by several Provided operations of an object that controls a piece of special hardware.

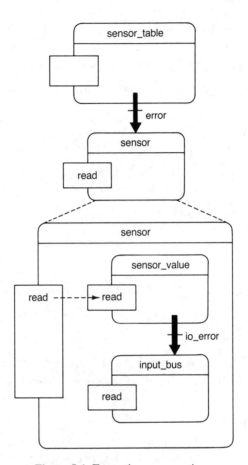

Figure 5.1 Exception propagation.

EXCEPTIONS

For a parent object, each exception in the Provided interface is mapped onto a child object Provided exception as follows:

Exception IMPLEMENTED_BY Object.Exception

As an example, let us consider the fragment of design shown in the HOOD diagrams in Figure 5.1. The object **sensor_table** uses the object **sensor**, and an exception **error** is raised by **sensor** and propagated to **sensor_table**. The object **sensor** is decomposed into objects **sensor_value** and **input_bus**, with exception **io_error** being raised by **input_bus**. The ODS of the object **sensor** could look like this:

OBJECT sensor IS

. . .

INTERNALS

. . .

EXCEPTIONS
    error IMPLEMENTED_BY input_bus.io_error;

. . .

END_OBJECT sensor

This would imply that **sensor_value** does not handle the exception **io_error**, which is therefore propagated as **sensor.error** to **sensor_table**.

An alternative is that **sensor_value** does not handle the exception **io_error**, but raises another exception **io_error_2** so that the ODS must be changed to read:

OBJECT sensor IS

. . .

INTERNALS

. . .

EXCEPTIONS
    error IMPLEMENTED_BY sensor_value.io_error_2;

. . .

END_OBJECT sensor

DATA

We recall that the definition of an object included the statement that 'an object is a model that combines both data and operations on that data'. The Internals is the place to define that data, giving the type and the range of values.

For a terminal object, each data identifier is declared in the normal Ada syntax, using a type from the Provided interface or Internals of this object or a Provided type of another object which is declared in the Required interface. The data value may also be initialised. The declaration may optionally be supplemented by a text description in natural language giving the meanings of these values and their use. For example:

    value : sensor.reading_type := 0; --| value of sensor reading |--

The data declarations collected from all the objects in the system would provide a data dictionary.

5.8 OPERATION CONTROL STRUCTURE

The detailed design of an operation of a terminal object is defined in an Operation Control Structure (OPCS), which leads the designer from a description of the operation, through pseudocode to Ada source code.

OPERATION_CONTROL_STRUCTURES
-- operation_definitions for terminal objects

OPERATION Operation_name [(List of Parameter : Mode Type)]
                                        [RETURN Return Type]

DESCRIPTION
    Text description of operation

USED_OPERATIONS
    List of Object.Operation

PROPAGATED_EXCEPTIONS
    List of raised exceptions

HANDLED_EXCEPTIONS
    List of handled exceptions

PSEUDO_CODE
    Pseudocode description of logic of the operation

CODE
    Ada source code of the operation

END_OPERATION Operation_name

Each operation of a terminal object will have an Operation Control Structure which defines in detail the interface and logic of the operation.

OPERATION DECLARATION
The operation name and parameter list are declared in full in Ada syntax. The parameters of the operation are defined with parameter name, mode (i.e. IN, IN OUT or OUT), type. For example:

count (time : IN seconds; total : OUT seconds);

If an Ada function is required to be generated instead of an Ada procedure for an operation, then the keyword RETURN followed by the return type may be added to the operation declaration, and all parameters must be of mode IN. For example:

count (time : IN seconds) RETURN seconds;

DESCRIPTION
The next item is a natural language description of the operation, derived from the informal solution strategy in the HOOD Chapter Skeleton (Chapter 2, section 2.2), and extended with further design details. This description should be included as the first stage of refinement of the ODS, as soon as the object interface has been defined.

If at a later stage the object is decomposed, and the operation is then implemented by an operation of a child object, this description will disappear, and may be copied to the implementing operation of the child object. The description should also include the raised and handled exceptions.

USED OPERATIONS

The next item is a list of the operations of other objects that are used by this operation. Since the object needs to be made explicit, the dot notation <object.operation> is used. Each operation named must also be identified in the Required interface as a Required operation where the full parameter list is given. The toolset can check this interface data against the Provided interface of the named object in the HOOD design data model.

PROPAGATED EXCEPTIONS

The exceptions to be raised by the operation are listed.

HANDLED EXCEPTIONS

The exceptions to be handled by the operation are listed, followed by a text description of what is to be done by the exception handler.

PSEUDOCODE

As the next stage of refinement, which may be considered as detailed design, the designer creates a pseudocode description of the operation. This is more structured definition of the operation than the natural language description above, but may still be written in English or another language, using the structured constructs of the Ada languages where appropriate. This section serves as a design to be coded by the programmer (who may also be the designer), and is not intended to be compilable. Each of the Used operations should appear in the pseudocode. Guidelines for writing pseudocode are in section 5.9.

The pseudocode section can be as detailed as the designer wishes and as far as knowledge permits at any stage. Further refinement can take place up to the point of generating Ada code itself from the ODS.

CODE

The last item is the code section, which contains the Ada source code of the OPCS. The Ada code generator will copy this section into the procedure or function that represents this operation in the Ada source. In order to maintain consistency of design and Ada source code, it is recommended that the programmer uses this section for all source code changes during development testing. However, an alternative may be to reverse engineer the finished and debugged source back into the operation code section after testing, provided that there have been no structural or interface changes at the object level.

TERMINATION
Each OPCS is terminated by an END_OPERATION statement. The whole ODS is terminated by an END_OBJECT statement.

The completed ODS of a terminal object ends the HOOD design of that object and allows generation of Ada skeletons incorporating the OBCS and OPCS code sections by a HOOD toolset. Changes in these sections are to be expected during subsequent testing of the Ada programs.

Examples of each part of the ODS may be seen in the full HOOD design of a traffic lights system given in Appendix E.

5.9 PSEUDOCODE GUIDELINES

The pseudocode provides a transition from design to code and should be easily understandable by non-software staff, i.e. user or system staff. It should, therefore, be structured English, using the same language as the requirements wherever possible and relevant, for example:

>   for all entries in table loop

As the design progresses, the pseudocode can develop towards Ada, in the sense that whenever a logic construct is used, the Ada construct should be used instead of a construct similar to another language, or to no language, for example:

>   for j in table'range loop

is much better at the later stages than

>   do for j = 0 to 99

Pseudocode occurs in the OBCS of an active object, and in the OPCS code and exception handler. The purpose of the pseudocode is to record the design in such a way that the following hold:

1. It is clear that the pseudocode implements the requirements, therefore it must be understandable by people who are not software experts.
2. The coding can be done from it, so it must be precise enough for detailed design and coding.

Consequently, it is recommended that the pseudocode consists of statements in simple imperative English, connected by logic statements following Ada-like syntax.

During the early stages of the architectural design, at the higher levels of the hierarchy, objects are being defined and decomposed. Therefore the pseudocode is replaced by Implemented_By statements for OBCS and OPCS for all non-terminal objects. As each terminal object is reached, the OBCS or OPCS has to be defined in detail in pseudocode, and it is to this process that this section refers. In the subsequent Detailed Design phase, the OBCS and OPCS is converted into Ada source code, with the pseudocode turned into comments.

The pseudocode may contain declarations as well as code. Thus the CODE section may contain:

    <declarations>
    begin
    <code>

The following guidelines are recommended.

DECLARATIONS
Declarations should initially be linked to any existing data definitions from the requirement analysis phase. Any external data definitions should be documented separately.

Enumerated types should be used initially, since these are easily readable.

STATEMENTS
Statements should be clear and unambiguous, in a form that declares *what* has to be done rather than *how* it is to be done. The terminology of the requirement documents should be used as much as feasible. Examples of suitable levels of detail are:

    send message 'begin' to object command
    change state to enabled
    calculate delta position
    call operation time.reset
    raise exception timeout to object command

LOGIC CONSTRUCTS
Ada-like constructs should be used since these are precise, easily understandable, and directly convertible to code without misunderstanding. It is not necessary to put the exact punctuation for Ada, although the exact syntax is preferred to avoid ambiguity. These logic constructs are:

1. if <condition> then
        <statement(s)>
    else   -- optional
        <statement(s)>
    elsif <condition> then -- optional
        <statement(s)>
    end if

2. case <expression> is
        when <choice> =>
        <statement(s)>
    end case

3. <label>:
    [while <condition>] | [for <range>] loop
        <statement(s)>
    end loop <label>

Note that the range may be expressed informally, with preference on the logical aspects of the entity being processed, avoiding literals if possible, for example:

for all entries of list loop

4. exit [<label>] [when <condition>]

If **exit** is used, then it should *always* be named to avoid any risk of ambiguity, which implies that the corresponding loop should be named. Loops should also be named when nested more than two deep to avoid error and to enhance readability.

5. block

A declarative block should not generally be needed in the pseudocode since this is an implementation-level concept. However, it may be used if thought necessary.

Conditional entry call and timed entry call (see *Ada Reference Manual*, section 9.7) may be used, but must be carefully explained since the implications of these constructs are highly critical to the performance of the system.

TASK CONSTRUCTS
The following constructs may be used only in the OBCS, since they define the tasking mechanisms.

1. accept <operation>

The OBCS shall have an accept statement for each constrained operation, followed by the necessary actions.

2. select
        [when <condition> =>]
        accept <operation> do
            <statement(s)>   -- during rendezvous
        end
            <statement(s)>   -- after rendezvous
    or
            <select alternative>
        [else]
            <statement(s)>
    end select

The OBCS will generally contain one or more select statements, in which some or all of the accept statements for the entry points are embedded. A real-time program may also have a timed entry call, corresponding to a TOER (see Chapter 7).

ADA PRAGMA PRIORITY

If it is necessary to allocate a priority to an active object, this should be given in relative rather than absolute terms, e.g.

This object has higher priority than object ABC.

OBCS EXCEPTION HANDLER

Every OBCS should have an exception handler to ensure that the possibility of task failure is considered. Further, the handler should not attempt to propagate or raise an exception, otherwise the task containing the OBCS code would hang.

5.10 HOOD PRAGMAS
(Ref. *HRM 3.1.1*, section 14.1)

A HOOD pragma is a directive in the ODS to allow the designer to configure code generation or to help in documentation. A HOOD pragma thus provides additional functionality to allow the ODS to be extended by a HOOD toolset vendor for project or implementation reasons.

HOOD provides three standard pragmas:

1. PRAGMA HCS (chapter => <HOOD Chapter Name>)

    The purpose of this pragma is to identify a block of text in the ODS as corresponding to a specific chapter of the HOOD Chapter Skeleton, which is named as a parameter. The pragma allows the ODS to include all the data of a HOOD object, and to be the mechanism of portability between tools and platforms (see Chapter 10, section 10.4, and *HOOD Reference Manual Issue 3.1.1*, Appendix E). An example is:

    PRAGMA HCS (chapter => Informal Solution Strategy)

2. PRAGMA Target_language (name => <language>)

    The programming language for code generation is nominally Ada, but a code generator could also generate a program structure in other languages such as C++. In each case, the language-dependent sections of the ODS, such as type, parameter list, code should be written in the corresponding format, or an alternative transformation could be provided by a code generator. For example, the data declaration of an integer in Ada would be:

    type second is range 0..59;

    with a corresponding type in C or C++ being:

    int second;   /* no range */

An example of the pragma is:

PRAGMA Target_language (name => Ada)

In general, this book assumes that the target language is Ada. There is a brief discussion of object-oriented language support in Chapter 10, section 10.3.2.

3.   PRAGMA ALLOCATED_TO <Physical_node>

This pragma is used in the IMPLEMENTATION CONSTRAINTS field of a virtual node object to define the physical mapping (see *HOOD Reference Manual Issue 3.1.1*, Appendix F.2).

Issue 3.0 of the *HOOD Reference Manual* provides for two extra pragmas, which may be used in some HOOD toolsets.

4.   PRAGMA MAIN [<operation>]

This pragma is put in the ODS of the root object of the system, and causes the generation of a procedure MAIN_ABC for the root object 'ABC'. A Provided operation of the object may be specified as a parameter, in which case this procedure calls the named operation. An operation must be provided for a passive root object, in order to execute the program. An active root object does not need to be called since it will execute when it is elaborated. An example of the generated code is:

```
with ABC;
procedure MAIN_ABC is
begin
   ABC.operation;       -- optional for an active root
exception
   when others =>
      null;
end MAIN_ABC;
```

An Ada code generator may be requested to generate this procedure for any root object in the system configuration in order to create an Ada program. Alternatively, the Ada code generator may allow the programmer to provide this code by hand.

5.   PRAGMA EXCEPTION <procedure_name>

This pragma causes a procedure <procedure_name>, which must have two string IN parameters, to be used to handle otherwise unhandled exceptions. An example of the code generated is as follows:

```
when others =>
   <procedure_name> ("From: <object name>.<operation name>",
   EXCEPTION_LOG.exception_name);
```

EXCEPTION_LOG.exception_name is intended to be a function that returns the name of the current exception that has been raised but not yet handled. This, however, is not a standard Ada function and is not supported by most compilers. For this reason, the pragma has been deleted from *HOOD Reference Manual Issue 3.1.1.*

6

CLASS AND INSTANCE
OBJECTS

6.1 CLASS OBJECT DEVELOPMENT

The four main features of object-oriented systems are often defined as encapsulation, data abstraction, inheritance and polymorphism. We have seen how a HOOD object supports encapuslation by restricting the interface to an object primarily to the operations provided by the object, and supports data abstraction by providing the types for the encapsulated data with the object. HOOD does not provide a full support for inheritance, and supports polymorphism in the static sense of overloading of operation names in the same way as Ada. However, HOOD does provide a class object as a template from which other objects may be created in a design, similar to the Ada generic package.

A class object may be defined thus:

> A class object is a template or type to represent a reusable object, with a set of formal parameters of types, constants, operation_sets and operations.

A class object represents a reusable object. Ada has often been commended as a language for reuse, a language which provides the package as a component that can readily be used. However, it is much more powerful to think in terms of design components to reuse, such as a HOOD object. For reuse to be practicable, there must first be a component that is reusable, i.e. a component that is made in such a way that it is useful to reuse it, either because it is generally a very useful component, or because it can be easily tailored to a new application. Secondly, it must be possible for the designer to understand what the component does. Thirdly, the designer must be confident that the component will deliver what it promises: that it will work correctly and robustly.

Now any object may meet these requirements. The first requirement may be met because the object is generally useful, such as a list or table object, perhaps as an abstract data type, or because the object has been built as a component of an application which is typical of the applications of the project team or company that produced it. Secondly, the standard HOOD chapter format of documentation means that each object is fully documented, with interfaces and functionality well defined and complete. Thirdly, the quality of an object may be certified if the object is either a server object (so that it does not require the services of any other object) or if it is an agent or actor object that uses only other certified objects. The object may be developed under quality control, and may be fully tested as a black box, to give formal acceptance.

In addition, a class object provides an extension for reuse in that it may be designed with parameters. These parameters permit several versions derived from the class objects to be made which differ from each other in specific ways. These versions are called instance objects.

There are two major ways of approaching object-oriented design. One is the project approach which is that primarily adopted by the HOOD Basic Design Step, where a set of problem requirements is designed into a program. The second way is to look at the general problem domain, and to select objects from this domain that look useful for future applications. This is a more investment oriented approach, which is intended to produce more reusable objects or classes, but does not specifically produce a program. In practice, most designers are funded to produce a set of programs for a project, from which a useful set of reusable objects or classes may emerge. An important rider is that, in this context, reuse can and does occur in many forms within a project. A simple module may be used many times, data definitions may be reused in interfacing programs, and objects that control hardware interfaces may appear in several programs.

Both these ways of development may be used to produce class objects. In the design process of the Basic Design Step, the designer may recognise that two or more objects in the design could be better represented by instance objects of a class because there is sufficient commonality and potential for parameterisation. In this case, a class object may be designed independently, and then multiple instance objects may be included in the design.

In the application domain approach, a class object may be designed specifically as a root object in its own design for future use. The design process of the Basic Design Step is then modified to incorporate an instance object of the existing class object directly into the design.

6.2 CLASS OBJECTS
(Ref. *HRM 3.1.1*, section 9.1)

A class object may be designed in the same way as any Ada program, starting from a set of requirements. In this way, a class object has its own HOOD design tree, so that

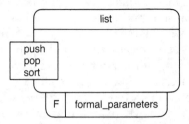

Figure 6.1 Class object **list**.

it exists as a design in its own right. However, there are some constraints, as well as the addition of parameters.

A class object may be decomposed into child objects. Any of these child objects may be an instance object of another class object. A class object may use another root object in the system configuration as an environment object. This allows a class object to be a template for an agent or actor object. A class object may be active or passive, and so child objects may also be active as well as passive.

A class object is represented in a HOOD diagram by an active or passive object with an uncle object box named **formal_parameters** attached (see Figure 6.1). Unlike a root object in a normal design, a class object diagram may well be empty, i.e. there are no child objects, since many of the most reusable class objects will be simple terminal objects such as data manipulation and storage objects like **stack**, **list**, **queue**, or else low-level hardware objects like **IO_bus**, **keyboard**, **screen**.

When a class object is decomposed into child objects, any of these descendants may require any of the formal parameters of the parent class object, so an entry is put in the REQUIRED_INTERFACE part of the ODS to list the required FORMAL_PARAMETERS (see *HOOD Reference Manual Issue 3.1.1*, section 12.12).

Figure 6.1 shows a simple example of a class object **list** with provided operations **push**, **pop** and **sort**, which has as formal parameters a type to represent the nature of each element in the set to be stored and sorted, and an operation **compare** which is dependent on the type.

A child object of a class object may use an environment object or it may use one or more of the formal parameters. This Use relationship must be shown as a Use link in the HOOD diagram. Figure 6.2 shows a more complex example. The class object is shown as being active, and has two child objects **child_1** and **child_2**; **child_1** is also shown as being active, and has two operations which implement the parent operations. **child_1** uses the environment object **object_e** and the other child object **child_2**. **child_2** uses the formal parameters, which means that **child_2** uses one of the operations specified as a formal parameter of the class.

The general form of the ODS for a class object is:

```
OBJECT Class_Name IS CLASS PASSIVE | ACTIVE
    FORMAL_PARAMETERS
    TYPES
```

List of ({Formal_Type_Declaration}
    added with textual description)
CONSTANTS
    List of ({Formal_Constant_Declaration}
    added with textual description)
OPERATION_SETS
    List of ({Formal_Operation_Set_Declaration}
    added with textual description)
OPERATIONS
    List of ({Formal_Operation_Declaration}
    added with textual description)
--| standard ODS
END_OBJECT Class_Name

Note that the textual description is optional. HOOD allows for an operation_set as a parameter of class and instance, but there is no natural mapping into Ada, so operation_set should not be used. It is expected that this parameter will be removed from HOOD in a later issue of the reference manual.

When a class object is decomposed into child objects, these child objects may in turn use one or more of the formal parameters of the class object. In this case, the ODS of the child object must declare these formal parameters in the Required interface section of its own ODS, which then automatically refer back to the formal parameters of the parent, or ancestor, class object.

Referring to Figure 6.2, the class object **active_class_name** could have its formal parameters defined in the Object Description Skeleton thus:

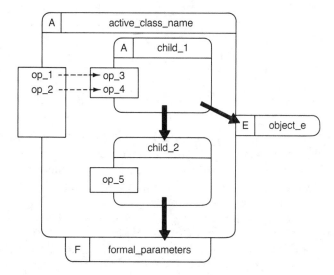

Figure 6.2 Class object.

```
OBJECT active_class_name IS CLASS ACTIVE
  FORMAL_PARAMETERS
    TYPES
      error_item
    CONSTANTS
      address
    OPERATION_SETS
      NONE
    OPERATIONS
      log_error (x : error_item);
--| standard ODS
END_OBJECT active_class_name
```

Object **child_2** would need to have a Required interface section in the ODS that looks like:

```
OBJECT child_2 IS PASSIVE
  . . .
REQUIRED_INTERFACE
  FORMAL_PARAMETERS
    TYPES
      error_item      -- name of type of Class Object
    CONSTANTS
      address         -- name of constant of Class Object
    OPERATION_SETS
      NONE
    OPERATIONS
      log_error;      -- name of operation of Class Object
  . . .
END_OBJECT child_2
```

6.3 INSTANCE OBJECTS
(Ref. *HRM 3.1.1*, section 9.2)

One of the options that a designer has when doing a Basic Design Step is to form an object as an instance object of an existing class object. Another option is to decide that an object has been designed sufficiently similarly to another object in the design that he should create a class object from them both, and then replace each object in the design by an instance object with suitable parameters. The instance object is then completely designed, equivalent to a terminal object in the HOOD design tree, even if the class object itself is decomposed into child objects.

An instance object may be created and used in any design from a class object by supplying a set of instance parameters for the class object. Instance parameters may consist of types, constants, operation_sets and operations.

The HOOD diagram form of an instance object is the same as a normal object, but the object name is followed by a colon and the name of the class object. Thus an instance object **message_list** of a class object **list** would be named as **message_list : list** in the HOOD diagram.

When the designer would like to have a set of instance objects derived from the same class object, then the HOOD diagram form may show this by using a double shaped or shadowed object, with the name turned into an array form. The number of instances to be created is repeated in the ODS of the instance object in a field called INSTANCE_ RANGE, which follows the name of the class object. In this way, a set of three instance objects of a class object **list** would be named as **message_list [1..3] : list** in the HOOD diagram, which would then represent three instance objects called respectively **message_list1**, **message_list2** and **message_list3**. This shorthand form could be used to provide lists to handle messages at three different priority levels, for example.

Another example of multiple instance objects is to provide a set of active objects to handle identical hardware devices asynchronously, such as a set of lifts. This is similar to providing a task type and multiple instances of the task, but it is done in a static way, so that a predefined number of active objects, and thus tasks, are created in the design process. To add another lift controller would require the designer to modify the HOOD diagram to increment the number of instance objects, modify any using objects to use the new object, and then to regenerate the code for these objects, compile the new package and recompile the modified package bodies.

Figure 6.3 shows an example of both forms of instance object in a HOOD diagram as described above. It is not necessary to show the environment objects used by the class object in the HOOD diagram that includes an instance object.

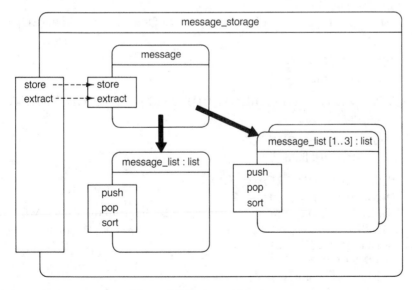

Figure 6.3 Instance object.

If an operation is provided as a formal parameter to the instance object, then it must necessarily be an operation of another object, since an operation can only exist as part of an object. Therefore, in this case, the other object should be shown as an uncle object of the object that includes the instance object.

The first part of the ODS declares the name of the class object, and supplies values for the formal parameters. The syntax and semantics of the formal parameters of the instance object must correspond to the formal parameters of the class object. The formal parameters may then be used in the Ada code generation to instantiate a package from the generic package corresponding to the class object. The remaining parts of the ODS may then be copied from the class object ODS, to provide an ODS that describes visible part of the instance object within the design.

The ODS for an instance object is:

```
OBJECT Instance_Name IS INSTANCE_OF Class_Name
        [INSTANCE_RANGE lower_bound . . . upper_ bound]

PARAMETERS
TYPES
List of {Formal_Type_Name => Object_Name.Actual_Type_Name}

CONSTANTS
List of {Formal_Constant_Name =>
        Object_Name.Actual_Constant_Name | Actual_Constant_Value}

OPERATION_SETS
List of {Formal_Op_set_Name => Object_Name.Actual_Op_set Name}

OPERATIONS
List of {Formal_Operation_Name = > Object_Name.Actual_Operation_
Name}

DESCRIPTION
    --| description |--

IMPLEMENTATION_OR_SYNCHRONISATION_CONSTRAINTS
    --| description |--

PROVIDED_INTERFACE
    --| standard fields |--

REQUIRED_INTERFACE
-- for all required objects |--
OBJECT Object_Name          --| Object_Name from the PARAMETERS |--
    TYPES
    List of (Type_Name)
    CONSTANTS
    List of (Constant_Name)
    OPERATION_SETS
```

List of (Operation_Set_Name)
OPERATIONS
List of (Operation_Name [list of (Parameter Mode : Type)])
EXCEPTIONS
List of (Received_Exception_Name)

DATAFLOWS
--| standard fields |--

EXCEPTION_FLOWS
--| standard fields |--

END_OBJECT Instance_Name

Each parameter may be followed by a textual description as an annotation enclosed between --| and |--.

6.4 EXAMPLES OF CLASS AND INSTANCE OBJECTS

COMMUNICATION SUBSYSTEM
As an example, it may be necessary to support two pieces of similar hardware, such as two radio sets for low and high frequency, and an intercom. We may then make a class object called **comms_link**, with instance objects **radio_lf** for low frequency, **radio_hf** for high frequency and **intercom**. The HOOD diagram is given in Figure 6.4.

OPERATOR TERMINALS
Another example is for the design to require two or more identical pieces of hardware at different addresses. In this case, a constant formal parameter could be supplied with the address.

The class object **operator_terminal** could be defined with the following ODS:

OBJECT Operator_Terminal IS CLASS PASSIVE
  FORMAL_PARAMETERS
    TYPES
      NONE
    CONSTANTS
      address
    OPERATION_SETS
      NONE
    OPERATIONS
      NONE
  --| standard ODS using the value of 'address' for the I/O |--
END_OBJECT Operator_Terminal

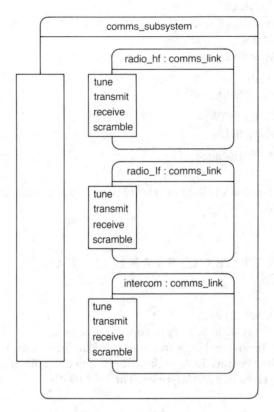

Figure 6.4 Communication subsystem.

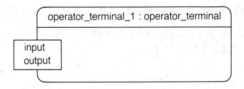

Figure 6.5 Operator terminals.

   The HOOD diagram is shown in Figure 6.5. There is no additional detail shown to distinguish the instance object from a normal object other than the name of the class object.

   An instance object **operator_terminal_1** at address 101 would be defined by the ODS:

OBJECT Operator_Terminal_1 IS INSTANCE_OF Operator_Terminal

  PARAMETERS
  TYPES
    NONE
  CONSTANTS
    address => 101
  OPERATION_SETS
    NONE
  OPERATIONS
    NONE

DESCRIPTION
  This object is an instance of the class Operator_Terminal to provide an interface to the operator terminal at the address 101.

IMPLEMENTATION_OR_SYNCHRONISATION_CONSTRAINTS
  --| standard fields |--

PROVIDED_INTERFACE
  --| standard fields |--

REQUIRED_INTERFACE
-- for all required objects |--

OBJECT Object_Name
  TYPES
    List of (Type_Name)
  CONSTANTS
    List of (Constant_Name)
  OPERATION_SETS
    List of (Operation_Set_Name)
  OPERATIONS
    List of (Operation_Name [(list of (Parameter Mode : Type))])
  EXCEPTIONS
    List of (Received_Exception_Name)

DATAFLOWS
  --| standard fields |--

EXCEPTION_FLOWS
  --| standard fields |--
--| no INTERNALS as these are the same as for the class ODS |--

END_OBJECT Operator_Terminal_1

6.5 STATIC OBJECT INHERITANCE

Although HOOD does not provide any specific support for class inheritance, in which a class can be defined as a specialisation of another class, retaining attributes and operations of the super-class and adding new attributes and operations of its own, there is a sense in which HOOD provides static inheritance of operations and types between objects.

This may be seen in essence in the Implemented_By relationship from parent operations to child operations. Since the parent object contains the child object, and there is a one-to-one mapping between parent operations and child operations, all the child operations that are required by the parent may be made visible in the parent interface by providing a corresponding Implemented_By link. This is seen clearly by looking at the Implemented_By link in the opposite direction, and by calling it an Inherits_From link. The same is true about types which are defined as IMPLEMENTED_BY in the ODS.

Thus static inheritance works in the opposite direction to hierarchical decomposition, and is therefore a bottom-up design process. This may be used to complement the top-down aspects of the HOOD Basic Design Step.

Figure 6.6 shows an example of static inheritance. An object **deposit_account** inherits the common operations **open**, **close** and **get_balance** from the more basic object **bank_account**, and in addition provides the operation **add_interest** which is implemented by the operation **add** of the new object **interest.**

The same technique can be used either to restrict access to an interface, by encapsulating an existing object that is to be reused inside another object with a similar but reduced interface, or to provide a means of renaming parts of the interface.

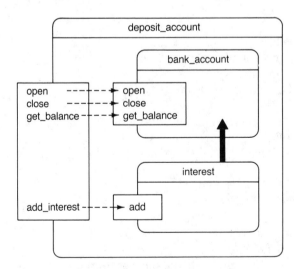

Figure 6.6 Static inheritance.

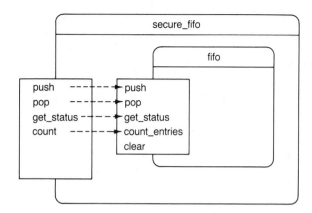

Figure 6.7 Interface restriction and renaming.

In the example in Figure 6.7, a new object **secure_fifo** is created that encapsulates reused object **fifo**, and inherits the operations **push**, **pop** and **get_status**, renames **count_entries** as **count**, and prohibits access to the operation **clear**, so that a user cannot clear the entries from the secure FIFO queue.

7

REAL-TIME DESIGN

On looking into the ways that HOOD supports the design of real-time software, it is worth first identifying the important characteristics of real-time software itself. Naturally, the key point is that real-time software should have a sufficiently quick response to any external event. Generally, this means either:

1. Providing a quick response to an interrupt, or
2. Being able to process all the data received sufficiently quickly, either:
   · to be able to command equipment quickly enough to control it, or
   · to be able to handle the next batch of input data in time before they are lost, overwritten or become out of date.

This response needs to be predictable, i.e. to happen reliably and consistently.

There are two major models for real-time design: synchronous and asynchronous. In the synchronous model, the software is divided into components, each of which has a time slice in which to run. If the allocated time is over-run, this is a serious design problem. Data acquisition is performed by polling, i.e. by reading data from registers on a regular basis.

In the asynchronous model, the software has components at different priorities, with the high-priority software dedicated to providing a quick response to external events, either interrupts or other forms of data entry, medium-priority software doing the normal processing, and low-priority software doing less essential tasks such as logging. If there is a temporary overload, then non-essential tasks are omitted for a time. Obviously, the design and system capacity should allow for all the work to be done on an average workload without any vital data being lost.

The asynchronous model is more able to handle unexpected overloads, but it is harder to test because there are more opportunities for variations and interactions between components at different priorities.

Ada supports both models, and therefore HOOD provides a notation to support both models too. The synchronous model makes no special demands, and can be provided purely by passive objects, or may use some of the features required for the asynchronous model. We discuss the way that HOOD supports the asynchronous model first, and then point to the subset needed for the synchronous model.

For a real-time system to deliver the required performance, several things need to be provided:

1. The hardware needs to provide data input/output channels, interrupts, memory and raw processing power of the CPU.
2. These need to be supported by the operating system or, in Ada systems, by the run time kernel.
3. The design method needs to support real-time concepts.
4. The programmer needs to code the programs efficiently.
5. The Ada compiler needs to compile the source code efficiently.

Thus while HOOD clearly has a role to play, the bottom line is that the computer processing power and memory must be adequate, the object code generated by the compiler good enough and the programming done well enough to provide a fast and reliable program. HOOD provides a method and some techniques to support and encourage this (active object, constrained operations, OBCS, and Op_Control object).

For the asynchronous model, HOOD provides the active object for concurrent execution, the constrained operation to give a rendezvous between concurrent tasks, and the asynchronous execution request (ASER) to support an interrupt.

For the synchronous model, HOOD provides the option to use these features (active object, constrained operation and ASER) as well as the purely passive object implementation. Since the main emphasis in the HOOD method is on the archi-tectural design aspects, with special stress on the interfaces between objects at an early stage, both in defining the interfaces and in checking the consistency between the Required and Provided interfaces of using and used objects, the main benefits may also be seen in the architecture of the design.

Thus HOOD provides a diagramming tool to express the structure of the concurrent tasks, the control flow between objects, the interacting operations, the data flow between objects, and the exceptions raised and handled. The Object Description Skeleton (ODS) provides a mechanism for expressing this further in the interface, and also in the Object Control Structure (OBCS) to define the interactions between the constrained operations in the object, and the Operation Control Structure (OPCS) to define the processing required for each constrained operation. This separation between constraints and processing is important in helping the designer to concentrate on the critical aspects individually, in helping the reviewer to see each in turn, and in offering a means for validating the interactions separately. In this regard, some work has been done in providing another means by using the Esterel language or petri nets to enable the OBCS content to be executed as a simulation before relying on the Ada source code being completed. However, a partial simulation can be done using a fully coded OBCS with appropriate stubs in the OPCSs to generate executable Ada code early in the development of the design.

A deadlock is when interactions between two tasks cause them both to be suspended due to a conflict in accessing a shared resource. One example is when two tasks both try to access the same two data items (with locks) in different orders. HOOD helps to prevent a deadlock happening by concentrating the early stages of design on the active objects and the interfaces between them. In this way, potential for deadlock can be seen early, and a prototype can be developed to validate the design.

HOOD helps to prevent closed loop execution or infinite recursion at the architectural level by prohibiting a cycle of Use between passive objects, and encouraging a seniority hierarchy. There is nothing that HOOD can do to prevent a closed loop in the code of a procedure itself.

7.1 CONCURRENCY

HOOD supports real-time design through a set of design concepts and notations that provide for concurrency and interrupts. Most of the code of most programs runs on a single control flow through a single processor, and HOOD provides a passive object for this sequential flow. A *passive object* is defined as an object to which control may be transferred from another object, causing an operation to be executed immediately. This corresponds to sequential processing.

Ada has been specifically designed for embedded systems which are characterised by interrupt driven, multitasking software. Thus to provide support for concurrency, HOOD defines another basic type of object.

An *active object* is defined as an object which contains its own control flow, and to which control is not transferred from another object, but which receives a stimulus to which it responds according to the internal state of the object.

The state transition of the object may be defined in the Object Control Structure in Ada semantics (task select and accept statements). An active object corresponds to an Ada task.

Active objects may provide an actor style in the design process, allowing the complex interactions of the design concurrency to be designed and modelled early in the design process, leaving the possibility of modification for tuning purposes at a later stage if the implementation reveals significant deviations from expected time allowances.

In the design process, the designer determines the type of object according to the needs of the external system. Thus, independent hardware devices may well be considered initially as needing to be supported by active objects, but it may be possible to simplify the design into more passive objects at a later stage to reduce concurrency overheads.

Note that Ada tasks may be considered to be less efficient in some implementations, and also less safe, which is an important point for safety-critical systems. Therefore the number of active objects should be reduced during the design process by transforming each one to a passive object unless there is a specific reason to keep the object active. Thus each active object in the final design needs explicit justification.

7.2 CONSTRAINED OPERATIONS

An operation of an active object may be said to be constrained if its response to its use by another object is constrained by the internal state of its own object. This corresponds to the way an entry point of an Ada task may be constrained by the task already being occupied with processing for another entry point, or be positioned in a select statement in a way that precludes immediate activation.

An operation is defined as being constrained by adding a trigger arrow to the operation name on the HOOD diagram (see Figure 7.1). This is simply a design notation to say that this operation is not a simple sequential flow to be executed immediately as soon as it is called but will depend on the internal execution state of the active object.

The way in which the operation is constrained is defined in a label on this trigger arrow. This label is then copied into the OBCS in the CONSTRAINED_ OPERATIONS section. This statement is used by the Ada code generation to create an entry point for the constrained operation. The label defines for the designer *how* the constraint is to be done, and this has to be written in more detail into the PSEUDO_CODE section of the OBCS. As a final step in the implementation, it has to be written in Ada by the programmer in the CODE section of the OBCS.

The label may be in any one of the following forms (see *HOOD Reference Manual Issue 3.1.1*, sections 3 and 12.5):

1. HSER = Highly synchronous execution request
   The using object is suspended until the execution of the constrained operation is complete. This corresponds to a normal Ada rendezvous. HSER should be used when the main purpose of the constrained operation is to return data.

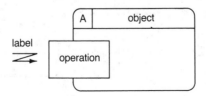

Figure 7.1 Constrained operation.

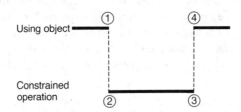

Figure 7.2 Highly synchronous execution request.

The HSER sequence is illustrated in Figure 7.2, which represents the processing timing of two concurrent processes: a using object and a constrained operation of another object. The using object processes until it calls the constrained operation at 1, when control is transferred to the constrained operation which then processes from 2 until 3. When the constrained operation completes processing, the original operation of the using object continues at 4.

2. LSER = Loosely synchronous execution request
    The using object is suspended until the parameters of the operation have been transferred to the constrained operation. This corresponds to an Ada rendezvous with acknowledgement. LSER may be used when a quick return to the using object is required with further processing, or when no data have to be returned.

The LSER sequence is illustrated in Figure 7.3, which represents the processing timing of two concurrent processes: a using object which is assumed to be of a higher priority than a constrained operation of another object. The using object processes until it calls the constrained operation at 1, when control is transferred at a rendezvous to the constrained operation which then processes from 2 until 3, at least in order to store the parameters of the call. When the constrained operation completes this initial processing, the original using object continues at 4 until the whole task represented by this control flow is suspended at 5. The constrained operation then continues execution at 6.

3. ASER = Asynchronous execution request
    All other objects are suspended until the constrained operation has

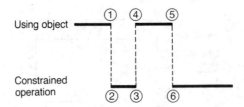

Figure 7.3 Loosely synchronous execution request.

been executed. This corresponds to an Ada task entry activated asynchronously by an event, i.e. hardware or software interrupt.

The ASER sequence is illustrated in Figure 7.4, which represents the processing timing of two concurrent processes: an object A and a constrained operation of another object. The object A processes until it is suspended by the interrupt at 1, when control is transferred to the constrained operation which then processes from 2 until 3. When the constrained operation completes processing, the original operation of the object A continues at 4. In this case, the constrained operation must be executing at a higher priority than object A.

4. ASER_by_IT<address> = ASER for interrupt

The ASER constrained operation is attached to the specified address of the interrupt by an Ada representation clause:

for <operation> use at <address>;

The ASER_by_IT<address> sequence is the same as that illustrated in Figure 7.4.

5. TOER = Timed out execution request

The constrained operation is defined to have a timeout duration attached so that if the constrained operation does not start execution within the time specified, then a Boolean called Timed-Out will be returned with the value True, otherwise if the execution call is processed (HSER) or acknowledged (LSER) within the specified time, then the Boolean called TimedOut will be returned with the value False. In this way, the designer may specify the timeout required in the HOOD diagram, so that it is passed through the design to the code. TOER may be used with HSER or LSER.

The TOER sequence is illustrated in Figure 7.5 in three examples. The using object processes until 1 when it calls the constrained operation with a timeout. In case A, the timeout elapses from 2 until 3, and the return to the using object has the Boolean TimedOut = True. In case B for an HSER, the rendezvous is made within the specified period, and the constrained operation processes from 4 until 5, then returns control to the using object at 8 with the Boolean TimedOut = False. In case C for an LSER, the rendezvous is again made

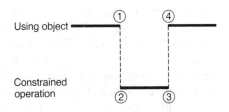

Figure 7.4 Asynchronous execution request.

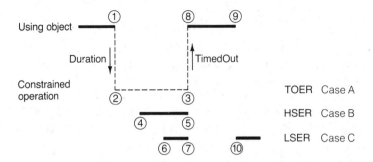

Figure 7.5 Timed out execution request.

within the specified period, and the constrained operation processes from 6 until 7, then returns control to the using object at 8 with the Boolean TimedOut = False, but when the using object completes at 9, the LSER constrained operation then processes from 10.

The label for a timed out execution request may denote a loosely synchronous or a highly synchronous execution request, as follows:

    LSER_TOER1.0   --| time out in 1.0 seconds |--
    HSER_TOER0.1   --| time out in 100 milliseconds |--

Note that if the target language is not Ada, then Ada specific remarks above should be reinterpreted in the light of that language. Specifically, a software interrupt may be implemented through an operating system service in a different way, e.g. Unix has a function kill() which may be used to send a signal from one process to another, causing a specified wait() to be woken up.

In Ada, entry calls to a task are queued on a FIFO basis, irrespective of calling task priorities. The time until the entry call is accepted is the time that a delay in a select statement applies to. Once an entry call is accepted (LSER or HSER), there is no control over how long the rendezvous and HSER execution takes. There is no means of timing out execution of an entry that has started in this way. Thus it is not possible to achieve hard real-time, deadline scheduling by this means. These restrictions are being addressed in Ada 9X.

FIFO QUEUE EXAMPLE

Figure 7.6 is an example of two objects combined to illustrate the use of the three main types of constrained operation. The senior object is an active object called interrupt which has two constrained operations called **handle_101** and **handle_102** which are, as might be expected, attached to interrupts at addresses 101 and 102. In order to ensure that no interrupt is missed, the data read by the interrupt handlers are stored in a FIFO queue by another active object called **FIFO_queue**. This object has a constrained operation called **add_entry** which is an LSER so that it returns control to the active object **interrupt** as soon as possible. **FIFO_queue** has another operation

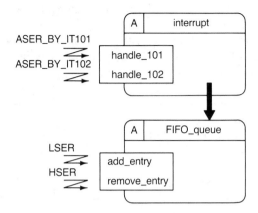

Figure 7.6 FIFO queue example.

called **remove_entry** which is an HSER since it has to return the data (there is no value in this operation returning control to a calling object without completing its processing of obtaining a value from the queue).

The OBCS for these objects is defined as an example in section 7.3 below.

7.3 OBJECT CONTROL STRUCTURE

7.3.1 OBCS definition

The logic of the relationship between constrained operations is defined in the Object Control Structure, which concentrates on the concurrent features of the HOOD design. The OBCS is in two parts, the first in the visible section of the Object Description Skeleton with the description and the constrained operations, and the second in the Internals with the logic of the OBCS.

OBJECT_CONTROL_STRUCTURE
    obcs_synchronisation in Visible section

DESCRIPTION
    text

CONSTRAINED_OPERATIONS
    List of Operations [CONSTRAINED_BY Label]

The description provides the first textual definition of the relationship between the constrained operations of the object. This will be further refined in the pseudocode and the Ada source code.

The list of constrained operations with the corresponding labels as defined in section 7.2 is generated from the HOOD diagram, or may be entered here and reverse engineered back into the HOOD diagram.

OBJECT_CONTROL_STRUCTURE
    obcs_implementation in the Internals

PSEUDO_CODE
    Pseudocode description of Object behaviour

CODE
    Source code in target language

IMPLEMENTED_BY
    List of Active Child Objects

The design of the OBCS really begins with the pseudocode description of the behaviour of the object. This may use a formal language such as Esterel, which may be executed as a simulation, or it may use a structured English (or other language) to define the interactions between the constrained operations. This section should be completed early in the design, during the architectural design, since the OBCS of the active objects is such an important and difficult part of the design of a real-time system.

The CODE section of the OBCS contains the Ada source code that implements the constraints. It is written using the Ada select, accept and other statements in the appropriate way.

HSER ADA CODE SECTION
The Ada code in the OBCS CODE section for an HSER operation called HSER_ OPERATION would look like this:

```
accept HSER_OPERATION (x : IN integer; y : IN OUT integer) do
    OPCS_HSER_OPERATION (x, y);
end HSER_OPERATION;
```

Here we see that the accept statement has two parameters, which are used as parameters in a call to the procedure OPCS_HSER_OPERATION. The rendezvous is not completed until the semi-colon following the procedure call, so the OPCS procedure is fully executed before returning control to the using object with the OUT parameter 'y' given a new value. This OPCS procedure has a name that is generated by prefixing 'OPCS_' to the operation name, and a body that is obtained from the CODE section of the corresponding Operation Control Structure:

```
procedure OPCS_HSER_OPERATION (x : IN integer; y : IN OUT integer)
is
   begin
      -- inserted OPCS CODE section
   end OPCS_HSER_OPERATION;
```

LSER ADA CODE SECTION

The Ada code in the OBCS CODE section for an LSER operation called LSER_OPERATION would look like this:

```
accept LSER_OPERATION (x : IN integer; y : IN integer) do
   begin
      x1 := x;
      y1 := y;
   end LSER_OPERATION;
   OPCS_LSER_OPERATION (x1, y1);
```

There will also need to be a statement that declares x1 and y1:

```
x1, y1 : integer;
```

Again we see that the accept statement has two parameters, which are used as parameters in a call to the procedure OPCS_LSER_OPERATION. And again the rendezvous is completed after the 'end LSER_OPERATION;' statement, but just before the procedure 'call', so returning control to the using object before the OPCS procedure is executed. Thus no parameters with OUT mode are possible for an LSER. The OPCS procedure is named and created in the same way as for HSER.

ASER ADA CODE SECTION

The Ada code in the OBCS CODE section for an ASER operation is similar to an HSER operation, except that generally there are no parameters since the ASER is responding to an interrupt. The ASER is expected to acquire the data from a register, buffer or other memory. Thus an ASER called ASER_OPERATION would look like this:

```
accept ASER_OPERATION;
OPCS_ASER_OPERATION;
```

Again the code of the OPCS is inserted into a procedure called OPCS_ASER_OPERATION with no parameters. Processing of the ASER requires the object containing the ASER to have a higher priority than the other ojects that are also enabled and ready.

TOER ADA CODE SECTION

A timed out execution request is complicated by the addition of parameters to signal the timeout duration and the success of the rendezvous. The Ada source code in the using object contains two data declarations:

```
d : DURATION;              -- predefined fixed point type for time
timed_out : BOOLEAN;       -- return value for success or failure
```

The code to call an operation with a timeout looks like:

```
TOER_object.TOER_OPERATION (x, y, d, timed_out);
if timed_out then
   -- perform error actions
else
   -- perform normal actions
end if;
```

This is implemented in the OBCS of TOER_object by the statement:

```
accept HSER_OPERATION (x : IN integer;
                       y : IN OUT integer;
                       d : IN DURATION;
                       t : OUT BOOLEAN) do
   OPCS_HSER_OPERATION (x, y, d, t);
end HSER_OPERATION;
```

The OPCS of the HSER operation can then be generated automatically to contain the code:

```
procedure OPCS_HSER_OPERATION (x : IN integer;
                               y : IN OUT integer;
                               d : IN DURATION :=
                                    label_default;
                               t : OUT BOOLEAN) is
begin
  t := FALSE;
  select
    begin
      OBCS.HSER_OPERATION       -- call to OBCS entry point
    end;
  or
    delay d;                    -- alternative delay
    t := TRUE;                  -- return value for timed_out
  end select;
end OPCS_HSER_OPERATION;
```

The default value of the timeout duration (label_default) may be taken from the TOER label attached to the trigger on the HOOD diagram. In this way, there is a standard default value for the timeout for this operation (**entry**), which may be overridden by a call from a using object.

   When an active object is a parent object, then the pseudocode and code sections are replaced by an Implemented_By section which contains a list of those child objects that are active, and that therefore contain an OBCS which provides the corresponding interactive constraints between the child constrained operations. This statement acts as a pointer to the reviewer of a HOOD design to find the next level of detail in the corresponding child objects.

In general, the OBCS is implemented by one or more child objects. However, there is a special case where a dedicated child object is created (as an active object) to handle the control flow interaction. In this case, the object may be named after the object itself, with a prefix of **CTRL_**, so that it is called **CTRL_**<object_name> (see *HOOD Reference Manaul Issue 3.1.1*, section 5.3).

7.3.2 FIFO queue example

Figure 7.6 shows a simple example of an object **interrupt** that handles two interrupts at addresses 101 and 102, transferring the data read into a FIFO queue. The OBCS part of the Object Description Skeleton for each object is shown below.

```
OBJECT Interrupt IS ACTIVE

    . . .
OBJECT_CONTROL_STRUCTURE

DESCRIPTION
    This object has two Constrained Operations to handle the Interrupts at
    addresses 101 and 102.

CONSTRAINED_OPERATIONS
    handle_101 CONSTRAINED_BY ASER_by_IT101;
    handle_102 CONSTRAINED_BY ASER_by_IT102;

PSEUDO_CODE
    Handle two interrupts (ASER_by_IT)
    loop on a select
        accept handle_101
        call OPCS for handle_101
    or
        accept handle_102
        call OPCS for handle_102
    end select loop

CODE
    loop
        select
            accept handle_101 do
                OPCS_handle_101;
            end handle_101;
```

```
    or
        accept handle_102 do
            OPCS_handle_102;
        end handle_102;
    end select;
end loop;
```

Each operation maps into a procedure called OPCS_handle_10X which will have a call to add an entry 'V' to the FIFO queue like:

```
FIFO_Queue.add_entry (V);
```

It is intended that other interrupts should be inhibited until this interrupt has been processed.

The OBCS for the object **FIFO_queue** is:

```
OBJECT FIFO_queue IS ACTIVE
    . . .
OBJECT_CONTROL_STRUCTURE

DESCRIPTION
    . . .

CONSTRAINED_OPERATIONS
    add_entry CONSTRAINED_BY LSER;
    remove_entry CONSTRAINED_BY HSER;

PSEUDO_CODE
    Two Booleans full and empty are declared in the INTERNALS.
    Declare a variable to save the parameter x.
    Loop on select for the operations:
        add_entry    : save x, end rendezvous, call OPCS
        remove_entry : call OPCS, end rendezvous

CODE
    begin
    x_save : value;
    loop
        select
            when not full =>       -- check if queue is full
                accept add_entry (x : IN value) do
                    x_save := x;
                end add_entry;        -- end of rendezvous for LSER
                OPCS_add_entry (x_save);
            or
```

```
              when not empty =>        -- check if queue is empty
                 accept remove_entry (x : OUT value) do
                    OPCS_remove_entry (x);
                 end remove_entry;      -- end of rendezvous for HSER
           end select;
        end loop;
```

The actual mechanics of adding and removing entries from the FIFO queue can be done in the OPCS without worrying about the interaction of constrained operations and the other tasking aspects. The full Object Description Skeletons of objects **interrupt** and **FIFO_queue** are shown in Appendix G.

7.3.3 HOOD tasking pragmas

HOOD Reference Manual Issue 3.0 provides three additional code generation pragmas which may be added to the CONSTRAINED_OPERATIONS field in the OBCS. These may be provided by some HOOD toolsets as an optional extension to HOOD for upward compatibility.

1. Pragma SERVER_TASK could be added to the definition of a specified constrained operation, and would cause an additional task to be created with a single entry for that operation.
2. Pragma GROUP could be added to the definition of two or more constrained operations in order to create an additional task with entries for the specified subset of constrained operations.
3. Pragma FIFO could be added to the definition of an ASER constrained operation, and would create three additional tasks in order to buffer the data received from the interrupt:
   · a server task to handle the interrupt;
   · a FIFO_queue task to store the data;
   · a consumer task to process the data.

Although useful, none of the features provided by these pragmas is essential. Indeed, having these extra tasks created by a pragma in the ODS conceals aspects of the implementation which one would like to see in the HOOD diagram. It is therefore recommended that additional tasks and a FIFO queue should always be created explicitly by creating a corresponding HOOD object in the appropriate HOOD diagram.

7.4 OP_CONTROL OBJECT
(Ref. *HRM 3.1.1*, sections 5.2.2 and 12.12)

One of the problems that was widely discussed in the development of the HOOD method was whether a parent object should necessarily be an empty shell: that is to say, its body should contain no operations and no data, and, as a consequence, each of its operations should be implemented by an operation of a child object. The HOOD Working Group decided that, for reasons of consistency, the parent object should always be an empty shell, and should therefore be limited to providing structure to the design. The alternative view would allow an operation of a parent object to contain code, and would be a more flexible approach, more consistent with normal Ada practice, but requiring the reader of a design to look at all levels to understand the details (this approach is being adopted by some HOOD designers).

As a result, a solution is needed for cases where a parent operation is required to be implemented by more than one child operation (e.g. initialisation might be needed on a set of child objects). One could make the design decision that one of the objects would control this process, but this could add a set of Use links to the design that applied only to the initialisation step, which might therefore be rather misleading regarding the design as a whole in the normal execution mode. The solution that was developed is an Op_Control object: an object which has the same name as the parent operation whlch it implements, in the form:

<parent_operation_name>

This object then performs the logic to call several child operations or whatever else is necessary. The Op_Control object is then implemented in the Object Description Skeleton as an Operation Control Structure. The diagram for an Op_Control object is similar to the symbol for an object, but without the Provided interface box containing the names of the Provided operations (see Figures 7.7 and 7.8).

Figure 7.7 shows an extension to the traffic lights example with an additional operation **start** of the root object being implemented by the Op_Control object **start**, which then calls the operations of the child objects **traffic_sensors.start** to switch on the sensor equipment, and **lights.start** to set the lights to the initial conditions of road BD = red and road AC = green.

Another usage of an Op_Control object (see *HOOD Reference Manual Issue 3.1.1*, section 5.2.3) is to provide a means for a constrained operation to be implemented by an unconstrained operation, or vice versa. This is done through the Op_Control object which handles the control flow interaction.

One area where this object is useful is in allowing a passive object to include an active object. This might be relevant when a designer is working top-down and has designed a passive object, but there is in the library a similar active object that could be used. In this case, the passive object parent could include the active object as a child, and map the parent operations to the child constrained operations via an

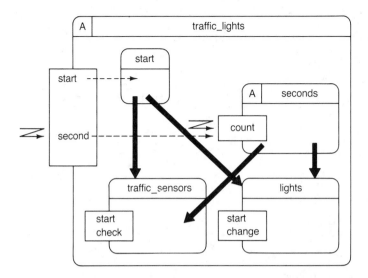

Figure 7.7 Traffic lights – Op_Control object **start**.

Op_Control object for each operation. This is illustrated in Figure 7.8, which shows a passive object called **passive_stack** containing an active object called **active_stack**. Two Op_Control objects called **push** and **pop** are created, so that the operation **push** of the parent object may be implemented by the Op_Control object **push**, and the operation **pop** of the parent object may be implemented by the Op_Control object **pop**.

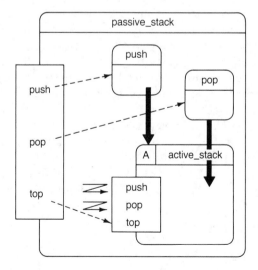

Figure 7.8 Passive object contains active object.

The Object Description Skeleton for an Op_Control object is:

OBJECT Op_Control_Name IS OP_CONTROL

DESCRIPTION
--| standard fields

IMPLEMENTATION_OR_SYNCHRONISATION_CONSTRAINTS
--| standard fields

PROVIDED_INTERFACE
NONE

REQUIRED_INTERFACE
--| standard fields

DATAFLOWS
--| standard fields

EXCEPTION_FLOWS
--| standard fields

INTERNALS
--| standard fields

OPERATION_CONTROL_STRUCTURES
--| a single operation
--| standard fields

END_OBJECT Op_Control_Name

The Provided interface is empty since it is always, in effect, a single pperation with the same name as the object. An Op_Control object is always a terminal object.

Examples of the Object Description Skeleton for the Op_Control objects **start** and **push** are shown in Appendix H. When you look at these examples, they are so simple that it seems to be inefficient to have Op_Control objects. In terms of executable code, there is no overhead compared with having an internal procedure for a parent object since the Ada mapping in both cases results in a procedure inside the package generated for the parent object.

The benefit of the Op_Control object is that the structure of the design is clearly visible where an Op_Control object is used, while the more general cases can be covered without using an Op_Control object. When an Op_Control object is not available in a HOOD toolset, another object with a single operation can be used, which only has the compile time overhead of an additional package.

8

ADA SOURCE CODE GENERATION

HOOD was originally conceived as an architectural design method, with Ada specifically in mind as the target programming language. As soon as HOOD was defined, it was clear that a set of CASE tools would be needed to aid in drawing and editing the HOOD diagrams, to help the designer to follow the HOOD method correctly, and to enforce the HOOD rules. Consequently, several HOOD toolsets have been developed with various names, and therefore this book, assumes that a designer will be working with a CASE tool. One of the benefits of a tool is that the whole design is available on the computer, and therefore it is possible to generate complete Ada programs directly from the HOOD design by creating a skeleton of Ada packages from the overall structure and incorporating the relevant declarations, definitions and code sections from the ODS where required.

This chapter describes the Ada mapping that is recommended, and the development process after completion of the design through the remainder of the implementation phase, i.e. coding and testing.

8.1 ADA CODE MAPPING
(Ref. *HRM 3.1.1*, section 14.2)

At the end of the HOOD design process, when the Basic Design Step has been performed on each object, the results are a HOOD design tree and a set of parent and terminal objects. Each of the parent objects has a set of entities that is implemented by child entities. Each of the terminal objects has a set of declarations, definitions and code sections which have been completed in Ada source code. The

Ada code generation process then produces a set of Ada package specification and bodies, and embeds the Ada source code that is in the Object Description Skeleton (ODS) into these Ada packages, thus producing compilable code files. Other information in the ODS may be included in the form of Ada comments, thus preserving the design documentation in the source code.

The Ada code mapping follows certain minimum rules called Kernel Extraction Rules defined in *HOOD Reference Manual Issue 3.1.1*, section 14.2.2. These rules are summarised in Table 8.1.

Table 8.1 ODS to Ada mapping

Object Description Skeleton	Ada
Object name	Package name
Passive object	Package specification and body
Active object	Task in a package
Operation (Provided and Internal)	Procedure or function declaration
Constrained operation	Procedure and entry point to a task
Operation set	Ada comment and set of operations
Use relationship	
= required objects	With package
Include relationship	
=internal child objects	With package
Exception	Exception declaration
Environment object	Package specification only
Op_Control object	Internal procedure in parent object
Class object	Generic package
Class object parameter	Generic formal parameter
Instance object	Instantiation of generic package
Provided type	Type in package specification
Provided constant	Constant in package specification
Internal type	Type declaration in package body
Internal data	Data declaration in package body
Internal constant	Constant declaration in package body
Type implemented by	Subtype of child type
Constant implemented by	Constant renames child constant
Operation Implemented_By	Renames procedure or function
Exception Implemented_By	Exception renames child exception
OBCS code section	Body of task
OPCS code section	Body of procedure or function
ODS section	**Ada comment**
DESCRIPTION informal text	Ada comment
CONSTRAINTS informal text	Ada comment
MEMBER_OF	Ada comment
RAISED_BY	Ada comment
CONSTRAINED_BY	Ada comment
Required interface	Ada comment
Data flow	Ada comment
Exception flow	Ada comment
OBCS description section	Ada comment
OBCS constrained operation	Ada comment
OBCS Pseudocode section	Ada comment
OBCS Implemented_By section	Ada comment

OPCS description section	Ada comment
OPCS used_operation	Ada comment
OPCS propagated_exception	Ada comment
OPCS handled_exception	Ada comment
OPCS pseudocode section	Ada comment

An Ada code generator may provide additional features. For example, *HOOD Reference Manual Issue 3.0* proposed that the operations could be generated as procedures that were *separate* from the packages to which they belonged, and that the task generated from an OBCS could also be *separate* from the package, each as an option that can be specified in the ODS for each operation in the OPCS and for the OBCS.

Another option was to permit the Implemented_By mapping for a parent operation to be performed either as a *rename* of the child operation, or as a procedure call to the child operation as the single statement inside an otherwise empty procedure.

The essential parts of code generation into Ada can be split into the following simple rules. These are illustrated with fragments from the traffic lights system design, which is provided in full in Appendix E as a sample design, with the corresponding generated Ada source. Note that there are two versions. The simple version does not have a class object, and in the second version, a class object is created for lights, so that two instance objects, **lights_ac** and **lights_bd**, can be made:

1. A passive or active object maps into a package specification and a package body called by the name of the object.
2. An unconstrained operation maps into a procedure, or into a function if there is a return type.
3. All items in the Provided interface are put into the package specification and body.
4. All items in the Internals are put into the package body only.
5. An OPCS code section is put into a procedure or function body:

```
with traffic_lights;
package traffic_sensors is
    subtype present is boolean;
    procedure check (road_name : in traffic_lights.road;
                     is_present : in out present);
end traffic_sensors;

package body traffic_sensors is
type address is range 1..4;
ac_sensors : array (1..2) of address := (1, 2);
bd_sensors : array (1..2) of address := (3, 4);
function read_sensor (sensor_address : IN address) RETURN present is
--H For this simulation, always return the value TRUE.
--H
```

```
begin
   return TRUE;
end read_sensor;

procedure check (road_name : in traffic_lights.road;
                        is_present : in out present) is
begin
--H PSEUDOCODE
   code;
end check;

end traffic_sensors;
```

6. An active object maps into a package containing a task.
7. The OBCS task is made visible to allow the operation to rename an entry.
8. The OBCS CODE section is put into a task body.
9. A constrained operation maps into a procedure that renames an entry point of a task:

```
--H OBCS specification
--H
task OBCS is
   entry count;
end OBCS;
--H operation renames entry point in task OCBS
--H
procedure count renames OBCS.count;

--H OBCS body
--H
task body OBCS is
--H PSEUDO_CODE
--H loop
--H    select
--H       accept COUNT and call its OPCS
--H    end select;
--H end loop:
--H
begin
   loop
      select
         accept COUNT do
            OPCS_COUNT;
         end COUNT;
      end select;
   end loop;
end OBCS;
```

10. A class object maps into a generic package with formal parameters:

```
--H package specification
with traffic_lights;
with text_io;
generic
   type road is (<>);
   road_name : road;
   procedure set_other_road (x : IN road);

package lights is
   Type colour IS (red, red_amber, green, amber);
   procedure change (to_colour : IN colour);
end lights;
```

11. An instance object **Instance_name** maps into a library unit as an instantiation of the generic package **Class_name** created from the class object, also called **Class_name**:

```
package Instance_name is new Class_name (parameter_1);
```

12. An environment object maps into a package specification which is sufficient to compile the objects that use the environment object, but not sufficient to execute the object – for testing, a body will have to be supplied, either a simulation or the real thing:

```
package Environment_Object is
   procedure Provided_Operation;
end Environment_Object;
```

13. An Op_Control object called **Operation_1** maps into an internal procedure in the package of the parent object:

```
package body Parent_Object is
   procedure Operation_1 is
   begin
      code;
   end Operation_1;
end Parent_Object;
```

14. The Implemented_By clause for types maps the type of the parent object into a subtype of the type of the child object.

15. The Implemened_By clause for constants, operations and exceptions map into corresponding **renames** clauses, these Implemented_By clauses may be illustrated by the package specifications of the following child and parent objects:

```
package child is
   type a_type is new integer;              -- define a type
```

```
a_constant : constant a_type := 9;        -- define a constant
procedure operation (x : IN a_type);      -- define an operation
an_exception : exception;                  -- define an exception
end child;

with child;
package parent is
    subtype parent_type is child.a_type;   -- create a parent subtype
    parent_constant : parent_type renames child.a_constant;
                                            -- rename the constant
    procedure parent_operation (x : IN parent_type)
        renames child.operation;           -- rename the operation
    parent_exception : exception renames child.an_exception;
                                            -- rename the exception
end parent;
```

An operation_set is simply a shorthand notation for several operations. It is expanded into the set of operations specified in the relevant child objects, each of which then renames the corresponding operation of a child object. The operation_set text in the ODS may be retained in the code as a comment.

In addition, it is necessary to provide visibility between packages so that Implemented_By (rename) and Use (operation calls) are possible. This is done by generating a context clause for each Required object and each Internal object:

```
with <Required Object>;
with <Internal Object>;
```

No Use clause is generated for any other package, since most Ada coding standards prefer the name of the package to be coded specifically each time.

The code generation process may have options to generate separate subunit files for the various subprograms. Possible options are:

· operations as separate procedures or functions;
· task as separate body.

Examples of Ada code generation for different types of object are shown in Appendices E and F. Appendix E is the full HOOD Design Document of a simple simulation of a traffic lights system. The object **traffic_lights** is a parent active object with Implemented_By links; object **seconds** is a terminal active object with an OBCS, and also uses other objects; objects **lights** and **traffic_sensors** are terminal passive objects. Object **traffic_sensors** also has an internal operation called **read_sensor**. Appendix F is the ODS and Ada code of an alternative design with object **lights** as a class object, from which two instance objects, **lights_ac** and **lights_bd**, are produced. Again, the corresponding Ada source code is shown.

8.2 VISIBILITY AND SCOPE
(Ref. *HRM 3.1.1*, section 13)

8.2.1 Visibility inside and between objects

Table 8.2 shows the visibility of the various parts of an ODS of an object from other parts of the same ODS for a terminal object; Table 8.3 shows the visibility for a non-terminal object, and Table 8.4 shows the visibility between ODSs of different objects. By visibility, we mean the ability of a declaration of an entity in one section of the ODS to refer to a declaration of another entity in the same or another section of the ODS. Any entity that has been declared in a Provided interface or Internals section of the ODS is visible to any of the following entity declarations in the same section.

Table 8.2 Visibility in a terminal object

Entities in ODS section	are visible in	ODS section
Provided interface	$\longrightarrow$	OBCS Internals OPCS
Required interface OBCS	$\longrightarrow$ $\longrightarrow$	Whole object Provided interface Required interface Internals OPCS
Internals	$\longrightarrow$	OBCS OPCS
OPCS	$\longrightarrow$	OBCS

Table 8.3 Visibility in a non-terminal object

Entities in ODS	are visible in	ODS
Provided interface	$\longrightarrow$	OBCS
Required interface	$\longrightarrow$	Whole object
Required interface OBCS	$\longrightarrow$	Provided interface OBCS Child object Required interface
Child object Required interface	$\longrightarrow$	Required interface
Child object provided interface	$\longrightarrow$	Provided interface OBCS

Table 8.4 Visibility between objects

From ODS section		To ODS section
Required interface	$\longrightarrow$	Class object Provided interface Environment object Provided interface Brother object Provided interface Parent object Provided interface

8.2.2 Scope

The scope of an object may be defined as those objects whose Provided interface is visible to the object. The scope consists of:

1. All class objects in the system configuration.
2. All root objects in the system configuration which may be seen as environment objects.
3. All brother and uncle objects in the same HOOD design tree.

Any of these objects may be made visible by being declared in the Required interface of the ODS.

8.3 CODE IMPLEMENTATION PROCESS

The generated Ada source code should be stored in a separate directory, from which it may be compiled into an Ada library. The Ada may then be tested from this library. The Ada source code may be edited to correct errors with a standard editor and may be retested, or parts of the ODS may be edited and the code regenerated from the design to preserve the coherence of the design and running code. The choice depends partly on the performance and availability of editors and HOOD tools, as well as the configuration control requirements. The preference is to maintain the design continually in step with the code being tested, because once a change is made to the code under test that is not in the HOOD design, there is a real risk that the correction will not be made successfully to the HOOD. In any case, it is necessary to maintain the interfaces to the objects in each ODS. There seems to be two viable strategies.

The first and best strategy is to maintain all the Ada source code of the HOOD design in the Object Description Skeleton, using a HOOD toolset exclusively for changes so that the Ada source code may be regenerated from the HOOD design after each set of changes. This strategy requires a good editor in the HOOD toolset, in order to be able to edit the different parts of the ODS quickly and correctly. It also requires a rapid code generator, which is not difficult to do because it is simply a question of remapping the contents of the ODS into a different format, i.e. in Ada packages instead of an ODS. It is also greatly improved by having options to minimise Ada source code regeneration and recompilation, such as a Make file facility, so that new Ada is generated only where changes to the corresponding parts of the ODS have been made, and Ada is compiled only when it has changed, or when one or more compilation units on which it is dependent have been changed and recompiled.

The second strategy is to use HOOD down to the pseudocode level, and maintain a separate set of Ada source files, originally generated from these Object Description Skeletons, but edited, compiled and tested independently. This has the disadvantage of separating the design from the coding. A separate effort is needed to ensure that the HOOD design is updated when the object structure, interfaces or pseudocode change. The possible advantages are that a language-sensitive editor may be used, or a less sophisticated, and therefore cheaper, terminal may be used for this stage which is purely text manipulation. The design could be recovered from the code at the end of testing by a reverse engineering tool. If the overall structure has not been changed, the existing design could be patched. If the structure has been changed, a completely new design or some new objects would be needed, thus losing the text chapters of the HOOD Chapter Skeleton.

The second approach is necessary when a programming language other than Ada is being used, for which there may be no corresponding source code generator.

It is recommended that the option for a separate compilation subunit for an operation is used during initial testing to reduce the recompilation overhead when changes are made to the code of an operation without changing the interface (i.e. procedure or function declaration). Later, when the operation has been debugged, the Ada source code for the object should be regenerated as a single source file to reduce the number of files to be maintained and the configuration management overhead.

An object provides an excellent entity for black box testing, since there has been significant emphasis on the early definition of the interface to the object. Therefore a bottom-up strategy is the most obvious. This strategy starts with server terminal objects, and then works up the seniority hierarchy until a complete hierarchy at this level is tested. The parent of the hierarchy can then be tested as it is the sum of its children. This strategy can then be followed up the tree until the root object is reached.

When an object has an internal operation, it may be possible to devise a complete set of tests that will adequately cover all cases for this operation in the context of the object, or it may be considered necessary to add the operation to the Provided interface temporarily for the purposes of testing only. This is the same problem as one would have when deciding how to test an Ada package that contains a procedure in the package body which is not declared in the package specification.

Any environment objects that are required for testing must be simulated if the fully defined object or the corresponding Ada packages are not available in time.

A class object can be tested only by creating several instance objects with it, and then testing those. For a project, it may be sufficient to test the class object with sets of parameters that correspond to the needs of the project, essentially testing only the instance objects. But in order to ensure that the class object is of high enough quality to put in a reuse library, it will be necessary to test the class object with as wide a range of parameters as is likely to be met in the application domain as a whole. This is the same problem as how to test a generic package.

A virtual node object (VN) is a collection of child objects, each of which needs to be tested first. If there is a large enough host machine, it may be wise to test the whole program as a collection of VNs on one machine, or at least to test pairs of communicating VNs in this way. Again, the process of bottom-up testing will lead naturally to a group of VNs before the full configuration is tested on the target machines.

Where the lower-level objects are produced last, and may be delayed by the need to interface to newly developed hardware, then a top-down testing approach may be followed. This implies the creation of simulated low-level objects (or stubs) to complete the execution paths. In this case, the test plans should minimise the amount of extra code being written, and should plan to implement the basic functionality first, gradually adding to this additional features and error checking.

8.4 DESIGNING TYPES

8.4.1 Defining types

The process of defining the types for an Ada program is one of the key features of the design process. This is especially true for an object-oriented approach, because the essence of the term 'object-oriented' is that the data are encapsulated in the object with the necessary operations, and that each data item *is accompanied by the types that define the data.* Thus the types themselves should be defined with the data, and then be made visible either through visibility of the object to the other objects that use it, or through the parent object. In the same way that an operation of a parent object can be implemented by an operation of a child object, so a type of a parent object can be implemented by a type of a child object, thus providing visibility of the child type at the level of the parent object interface. This 'implemented by' process can be repeated up the HOOD design tree wherever necessary.

Designing types may be done from the top down, or from the bottom up. In other words, the definition of a type may be done when the object is first identified to exist as part of the initial design, or the definition of all types may be left until the full HOOD design tree has been produced, and the terminal objects identified.

The definition of each type must be given in a terminal object, in either the Provided interface or the Internals. This definition may then be referenced from a parent object using the Implemented_By clause in the Internals of the parent object. Alternatively, the type may initially be named in the parent object before decomposition, and then referenced using the Implemented_By clause and defined in the child object after decomposition.

Additional types that are not needed to be visible outside the object may be declared fully in the Internals. Any Ada type may be defined in the Proided interface and Internals except a task type, which is described in section 8.4.4.

8.4.2 Types of types

A type declaration may appear in full in the Object Description Skeleton in the Provided interface or Internals as follows:

TYPES
    DAYS is (Sun, Mon, Tues, Wed, Thurs, Fri, Sat);

The *HOOD Reference Manual Issue 3.1.1* specifically permits and requires a type declaration to follow the rules of the target language, which in this case is Ada. The *Ada Language Reference Manual* section 3.3.1 specifies the following type definitions, which are given here with a simple example:

- enumeration
    type DAYS is (Sun, Mon, Tues, Wed, Thurs, Fri, Sat);

- integer
    type DAY is range 1..7;

- real
    type TEMPERATURE is digits 4;
    type AMP is delta 0.1 range 0.0 .. 10.0;

- array
    type TEAM is array (1..TEAMSIZE) of PLAYER;

- record
    type PLAYER is
      record
        NUMBER : T_NUMBER;
        POSITION : T_POSITION;
        NAME   : STRING (1..20);
      end record;

- access
    type POINTER is access DRAWER;

- derived
    type AGE is new INTEGER;

- incomplete
    type SECRET;

- private
    type MONEY is private;
    type SPENDING_MONEY is limited private;

Subtypes are treated separately in the *Ada Language Reference Manual* section 3.3.2 with the syntax:

subtype <identifier> is <subtype_indication>;

where <subtype_indication> is a type or subtype followed by an optional constraint.

HOOD does allow a subtype definition in the Provided interface or Internals. Whereas it would seem that an object should have a full type definition, it is too restrictive to prohibit a subtype of another type, such as a standard type; and a subtype also provides an Implemented_By mapping for types.

The problem of the different styles of type definitions can be resolved by a HOOD toolset by looking at the first token after the keyword 'is' in the type or subtype definition. If the token is an Ada keyword or an opening parenthesis for an enumeration type, then the definition is a type definition, otherwise the definition is a subtype definition. Thus we have three simple cases – the first two become Ada types:

DAY is range 1..7;   => type DAYS is range 1..7;

DAYS is (Sun, Mon, Tues, Wed, Thurs, Fri, Sat); =>
        type DAYS is (Sun, Mon, Tues, Wed, Thurs, Fri, Sat);

The next becomes an Ada subtype:

DAY is INTEGER range 1..7; => subtype DAYS is INTEGER range 1..7;

The relevant keywords are:

access	limited	record
array	new	(
delta	private	
digits	range	

Note that the syntax for a task type is different and is not allowed in a Provided interface or Internals:

```
task type T is
   entry E;
end T;
```

A type may be fully defined in the Provided interface in which case it is fully visible to a using object. An incomplete type may be named in the Provided interface and be completed in the Internals.

A private type is declared in the Provided interface, and is then completed in the Internals. A private type is only permitted for a terminal object.

8.4.3 Mixed declarations of types and constants

It is common practice to use a constant in defining a type, for example the size of an array may be given in this way so that the size can be used in several places:

```
TEAMSIZE : constant integer := 11;
type T_NUMBER is range 1..TEAMSIZE;
type T_POSITION is (goalkeeper..left_wing);
type PLAYER is
   record
      NUMBER  : T_NUMBER;
      POSITION : T_POSITION;
      NAME     : STRING (1..20);
   end record;
type TEAM is array (1..TEAMSIZE) of PLAYER;
```

Therefore the HOOD ODS has the flexibility to allow this mix. The BNF of the Object Description Skeleton in the *HOOD Reference Manual Issue 3.1.1*, Appendix C allows for flexibility, whereas the sample outline of an ODS for each type of object in *Issue 3.1.1*, section 12 shows a possible format.

8.4.4 Task types

A task type is a template for a process (task) that can be created many times, each time the same way, each with its own associated data:

task type = types + data + operations + control flow

The syntax for a task type is:

```
task type T is
   entry E;
end T;
```

Although task types cannot be exported from a HOOD object, there is no restriction on the provision of a task type within an object, so that we may design an active object in the normal way as an object with its own control flow, and this may be implemented as a set of tasks of varying dimension, by dynamically creating each task as and when it is needed. The use of a task type in the active object should be defined in the Object Description Skeleton in the OBCS. The rationale for this approach is that:

1. The essence of object oriented design is that data are encapsulated in an object and accessed by the operations of the object. Exporting a task type is to export a template for a control flow and is more like exporting a class object itself.
2. An active class object provides the capability for multiple instances of a task.

3. A task type in an active object provides the needed facility, but lacks explicit visibility of the multiple and dynamic nature of the active object. This visibility could be provided by giving a plural name, and the name and purpose of the task type must be clearly spelt out in the Object Description Skeleton.

OBJECT aircraft_tracks IS ACTIVE
DESCRIPTION
    The object aircraft_tracks has a dynamic representation of the aircraft tracks detected by the radar.
    Each aircraft track is represented by an instance of a task type aircraft_track which is defined in the OBCS.

    . . .

OBJECT_CONTROL_STRUCTURE

    . . .

CODE
    task type aircraft_track is
        entry reposition (x, y, z);
    end aircraft_track;

    task body aircraft_track is
    begin
        accept reposition (x, y, z) do

        . . .

        end reposition;
    end aircraft_track;

9

DISTRIBUTED SOFTWARE DESIGN

9.1 VIRTUAL NODE OBJECT
(Ref. *HRM 3.1.1*, section 11 and Appendix F)

Most aerospace and military embedded systems have more than one processor. Many space satellite systems have as many as ten processors when experiment processors are included. The Columbus Manned Space Station has a local area network with four system processors and further experiment processors. Since it is now common that Ada software has to be designed to run on a set of processors, HOOD provides a virtual node object (VN) to tackle the concept of distribution in Ada software. Indeed, this fact has now been recognised by additions to the Ada language in Ada 9X to provide for distribution directly.

The program for a distributed system is designed as a set of virtual node objects, in which each VN communicates with other VNs without regard to which processor that VN or the other VNs are running on. A subsequent design activity assigns each VN to a processor, leaving the distributed operating system to provide suitable connectivity. In order to support this concept, there are certain features of a virtual node object:

1. Each VN is an active object, so that it has its own control flow, and may be moved freely from one processor to another.
2. A VN can provide only constrained operations, since there can be no sequential processing across processor boundaries.
3. A Use relationship between two VNs may be supported by several different mechanisms for communication within or between processors, including some of:
   · local rendezvous within a processor following Ada protocol;
   · remote rendezvous between processors, supported by a distributed operating system to provide a transparent interface to the programmer, which looks like the Ada protocol;

- shared memory, using a signal between processors, or a data item in shared memory acting as a semaphore;
- message passing, in which a distributed operating system provides acknowledgement that a message has been passed to the correct destination and has been received correctly;
- message broadcast to several destination VNs, where the distributed operating system supports a list of VNs as destination for the message, and returns a list of acknowledgements to the sender;
- local area network, where a distributed operating system handles the protocol for the network.

4. A VN may be decomposed into other VNs only, in order to be distributed among processors.

5. A VN which is not decomposed into other VNs is called a terminal VN, and is decomposed into at least one active object and other active/passive objects as needed.

6. A VN can use only other VNs, since there are only VNs at the same level of decomposition. This is the level of distributed software.

7. A HOOD object may be duplicated in several terminal VNs. This appears to be contrary to the uniqueness rule that 'an object shall not have more than one parent' (see *HOOD Reference Manual Issue 3.1.1*, Appendix A.3, rule I–5), since a VN may be considered as a parent, and two VNs containing the same object may be loaded on the same processor. However, it should instead be seen as a modification to the rule specifically for VN objects. In Ada terms, part of the point of the uniqueness rule is to allow the object to map into an Ada package with a unique name as is required by the Ada compiler. However, when the same name is used for two objects, which are in fact the same object, then there is no ambiguity in the Ada compilation system, since one Ada package may be used to represent the HOOD object. Another solution is for the Ada package corresponding to the VN to encapsulate the code generated for the HOOD terminal objects allocated to it.

8. All types, constants and exceptions provided by a virtual node object shall be implemented by a child object. This follows automatically from the fact that a VN must be a parent object (see *HOOD Reference Manual Issue 3.1.1*, Appendix F, rules I–5 to I–9).

9.2 VIRTUAL NODE OBJECT DIAGRAM

A virtual node object diagram is represented by an object symbol with a 'V' in a box at the top left-hand corner, as shown in Figure 9.1.

In this example, there are two operations and one operation_set in the Provided interface. Each operation and each operation_set has a trigger arrow attached since all operations and operation_sets of a VN are constrained. There is also a label which

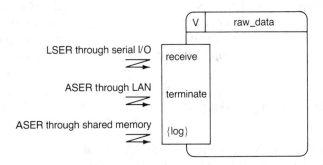

Figure 9.1 Virtual node object.

indicates the type of constraint and the communication protocol that supports use of the operation or operation_set. Thus the Provided interface of the virtual node object **raw_data** is:

- · Operation **receive** which is loosely synchronous through a serial link.
- · Operation **terminate** which responds to an asynchronous interrupt from the local area network.
- · Operation set {**log**}, which is used to set logging on and off to different sinks, and is triggered by one or more ASER interrupts to read data from shared memory.

HOOD Reference Manual Issue 3.1.1 implies that a trigger arrow label can be any one of ASER, LSER or HSER. The consequences may depend on whether the VNs are executing on the same processor, or on two different processors, as follows:

1. On the same processor:
   - · ASER implies an interrupt, so that the using VN can continue processing concurrently with the used VN. However, the VN that is mapped into the Ada task with the higher priority will in fact process – no parameters can be passed.
   - · LSER implies that the parameters of the operations are stored before returning control to the using VN.
   - · HSER implies that the used operation completes processing before returning control and response data to the using VN.
2. On two different processors:
   - · ASER implies an interrupt, so that the using VN can continue processing concurrently with the used VN – no data are passed in either direction.
   - · LSER implies that the parameters of the operations are stored before returning control to the using VN, which means that the using VN needs to be suspended until an acknowledge is received.
   - · HSER implies that the used operation completes processing before returning control and response data to the using VN, which means that the using VN needs to be suspended until a reply is received.

Trigger arrow	*Used VN*	*Using VN*
ASER	Concurrent	Concurrent
LSER	Saves data	Waits for acknowledge
HSER	Completes execution	Waits for reply

9.3 VIRTUAL NODE OBJECT ODS

OBJECT Virtual_Node_Name IS VIRTUAL_NODE
    [PRAGMA TARGET_LANGUAGE language]

DESCRIPTION
    object_description_text for Virtual Node Object

IMPLEMENTATION_OR_SYNCHRONISATION_CONSTRAINTS
    implementation_constraints_text
    [PRAGMA ALLOCATED_TO Physical_Node]

PROVIDED_INTERfACE
    provided_interface_definitions

REQUIRED_INTERFACE
    required_interface_definitions

DATAFLOWS
    dataflow_definitions

EXCEPTION_FLOWS
    exception_flow_definitions

OBJECT_CONTROL_STRUCTURE
    obcs_synchronisation

INTERNALS
    internal_definitions

OBJECT_CONTROL_STRUCTURE
    obcs_implementation

END_OBJECT Virtual_Node_Name

OBJECT DEFINITION
The object type is set to VIRTUAL_NODE. The DESCRIPTION section describes
the functionality of the VN, independent of its allocation to a specific physical node.
The IMPLEMENTATION_OR_SYNCHRONISATION_CONSTRAINTS sec-
tion describes the constraints on the operations overall by describing the meaning of
the labels on the triggers. For a communication protocol, reference may be made to
a relevant document. The rationale for the physical node allocation is given prior to

selection, and the justification for the selected physical node is given when the allocation has been made.

This section is also a suitable place for putting size and timing budgets, estimates and actual values. The pragma for allocation of a virtual node object to a physical node is:

PRAGMA ALLOCATED_TO Physical_Node

This pragma is inserted in the implementation constraints, and is used by the Ada code generation to collect together the VNs on each physical node into a single Ada program, with a name generated from the name of the physical node. The parameter Physical_Node should be a logical name, such as one of a set like:

P1, P2, P3
Input, Command, Console
Crew_Work_Station, Database, DMS, Experiment, Subsystem

PROVIDED INTERFACE

The Provided interface is similar to the standard ODS, but all the entities in the Provided interface are implemented by an allocated child object.

REQUIRED INTERFACE

The Required interface is similar to the standard ODS, giving the required entities for each used virtual node object.

DATA FLOWS AND EXCEPTION FLOWS

The data flows and exception flows are the same as the standard ODS.

OBJECT CONTROL STRUCTURE

The OBCS of a virtual node object is restricted to the interface or visible part only, containing the description and constrained operations. Since each operation is implemented by a child object, there is no need for PSEUDO_CODE or CODE sections.

An additional item for each constrained operation is the definition of the link protocol for each constrained operation, giving the following syntax:

CONSTRAINED_OPERATIONS
    List of Operations CONSTRAINED_BY Label THROUGH Protocol

The protocol is named in the syntax above, and in the DESCRIPTION section. It is either described in full, or a reference is given to a description elsewhere in the HOOD Design Document or in another document. The protocol must be supported by one or more HOOD objects, or by an underlying operating system.

INTERNALS

The Internals always contains a list of internal child virtual node objects or a list of allocated non-VN objects.

For each of the entities in the Provided interface, the Internals contains an Implemented_By statement, mapping the entity onto one of the Provided entities of a child VN or other object.

Note that a VN either contains and is decomposed into only VNs, or contains no VNs (i.e. it is a terminal virtual node object).

OPERATION CONTROL STRUCTURE

Since all the operations of a VN are implemented by a child object operation, there are no Operation Control Structures for a VN.

DEVELOPMENT OF THE OBJECT DESCRIPTION SKELETON

It is expected that the structural relationships between a virtual node object and its child objects, virtual node object or otherwise, will be created from the HOOD diagram of the VN. From this diagram, the ODS is created containing:

> The Virtual_Node_Name
> Provided operations and operation_sets
> Required object names
> Data flows
> Exception flows
> Internal object names
> Implemented_By links for operations and operation_sets

Subsequent refinement, therefore, consists of filling in details of:

> Description of the virtual node object
> Definition of constraints on each operation
> Definition of the communication protocols
> Names of Provided types, constants and exceptions
> Names of Required types, constants and exceptions
> Names of Required operations and operation_sets
> Description of the OBCS
> Name of protocol of each constrained operation
> Implemented_By mapping for each of the Provided entities

9.4 DESIGNING A PROGRAM WITH VIRTUAL NODE OBJECTS

APPROACH 1

The approach to developing a design of a distributed program that is described in *HOOD Reference Manual Issue 3.1.1* is first to develop a design as if the whole program is to run on one processor, thus arriving at a good set of objects, and then to allocate these objects to VNs. A major advantage of this approach is that the design process follows the HOOD Basic Design Steps in the normal way, and so the object orientedness of the design is preserved. This method can be summarised as:

1. Perform the HOOD design to produce a set of objects in a HOOD design tree.
2. Define a set of empty VNs, with at least one per processor.
3. Allocate objects to VNs by editing each VN HOOD diagram in turn to include selected object diagrams, and define the VN interface as the union of the interfaces of the objects allocated.
4. Allocate VNs to processors by inserting the pragma ALLOCATED_TO in the implementation constraints in the ODS.

The criteria to be used are:

1. Minimise communication between processors, using an analysis of data flow traffic between objects.
2. Create enough VNs to provide flexibility, so that if one processor becomes overloaded in memory or CPU usage, then a VN can be moved to another processor.
3. Software that has to be on a specific processor is isolated in a VN which is allocated to that processor, e.g. software to handle a piece of hardware that is connected directly to one processor only is constrained to reside on that processor.
4. Software that is free to migrate should not be unduly constrained to a specific processor. For example, if the system has a database to be managed, the low-level disk interface software needs to reside on the processor that is connected to the disk drive, but the logical database software need not necessarily be tied to that processor. Within the constraints of memory and processing power, the objective is to avoid high communication interface overheads.

APPROACH 2

Select each of the active objects, which are at the top-level of the HOOD design tree that was defined in the first stage above, as the controlling object of a virtual node object. Then each of the passive objects used directly or indirectly by an active object is incorporated into the VN of that active object, so that the VN contains all of the subtree necessary to be able to exist alone in a processor, or to be combined with one or more other VNs. These VNs are then allocated to processors as above.

If a natural single processor design does not produce enough active objects to create enough virtual node objects, then it will be necessary to create a VN out of a passive object. This approach is illustrated in Figure 9.2 in which two active objects, **actor_1** and **actor_2**, use two agent objects and two server objects. These objects may then be reorganised into two virtual node objects containing respectively:

actor_1, agent_1 and server_1
actor_2, agent_2, server_1 and server_2

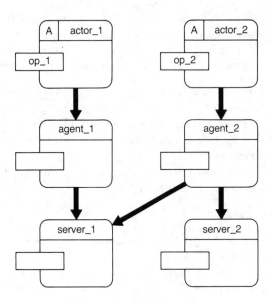

Figure 9.2 Active objects approach – objects.

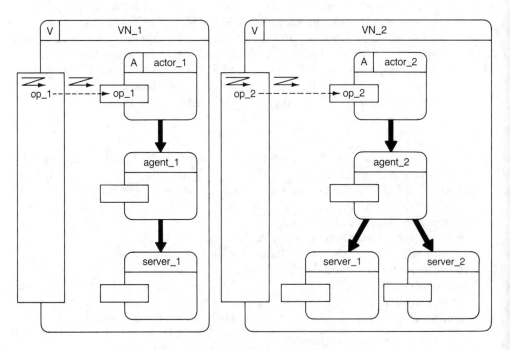

Figure 9.3 Active objects approach – VNs.

This is shown in Figure 9.3.

Note that each of the operations of the Provided interface of the two active objects is mapped onto the Provided interface of the corresponding parent virtual node object to allow communication between the active objects through the VN interfaces.

APPROACH 3

Another approach is to consider the design at the top level as a set of virtual node objects, using the HOOD Basic Design Step method. Each VN may then be decomposed in turn, either into further VNs, or into non-VN objects. The choice depends on whether there are already enough VNs to allow for a flexible system, whether the objects of the VN need to remain tightly bound in one processor, and whether there are naturally any more active objects to separate the control flows further. The criteria of approach 1 also apply. The main advantage of the third approach is that the distributed aspect is fully considered at the beginning of the design.

In any approach, it is always possible to change the type of an object to or from a VN at any stage. In all approaches, knowledge of the planned hardware and software system is required before a good set of virtual node objects can be defined. If, therefore, the hardware has not been defined when software design begins, in addition to be being able to influence the hardware designer into providing a suitable number of processors, the software designer needs to allow sufficient flexibility in the design to do the processor allocation later.

In these cases, approach 1 can easily be separated into two parts, leaving the virtual node object and processor allocation until the hardware configuration has been defined (likewise approach 2) and continue with a logical design. However, approach 3 is handicapped if the hardware configuration is not known, but, providing a reasonably reliable assumption can be made about the number and nature of processors that will available, this approach is flexible enough to postpone the processor allocation part without serious penalty.

Allocation of virtual node objects to processors may need to be revised when the software has been developed and the actual size and performance figures have been obtained. In addition, the traffic model that provides figures about the data flows through the system becomes more accurate as the project proceeds, and more attention is paid to this difficult and seemingly low-priority aspect of the design as real data become available.

Let us consider an example to see how virtual node objects may be created for a satellite software system. We may think of the software for a satellite as a set of functional subsystems, for example attitude control, thermal control, electrical power distribution and data management. In addition, there needs to be software to control the payload, either scientific experiments or a commercial payload such as communications equipment. So at the first level, these subsystems represent a breakdown of the satellite software system (Figure 9.4).

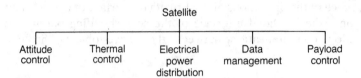

Figure 9.4 Satellite software system.

Each of these subsystems will, in turn, consist of software to acquire data, software to process data and software to output commands to the hardware as a result of this processing. Some of this software will be very complex, for example attitude control software. Other processing could be much simpler, such as monitoring temperature and electrical current values against sets of predefined limits.

The primary role of HOOD is as an architectural design method for structuring the software, so the structuring process is very similar from one subsystem to another. For example, we know that the satellite can receive commands over the telecommand link. The satellite software is decomposed so that the software then contains a telecommand object that has operations to receive telecommands and to process or distribute them to the appropriate objects. We may decompose the telecommand object into one object that is servicing the hardware of the telecommand link, that responds to interrupts, and receives and buffers the telecommands, a second object for telecommand processing decomposition, and perhaps further objects for different types of telecommand which are then responsible for controlling the hardware directly, for reconfiguring the system, and for reporting to the ground.

Let us assume that there will be three processors on the satellite, and because of the hardware configuration, the intention is for each to perform these functions:

1. One primarily available for attitude control.
2. One primarily a supervisor and for data management.
3. One primarily for thermal, electrical and payload control.

We may recognise that data management really has two parts, in addition to overall control:

1. Data input to the satellite via a telecommand link.
2. Data output from the satellite via a telemetry link.

We may then design seven virtual node objects as follows:

Attitude control
Thermal control
Electrical control
Data management control
Telecommand
Telemetry
Payload

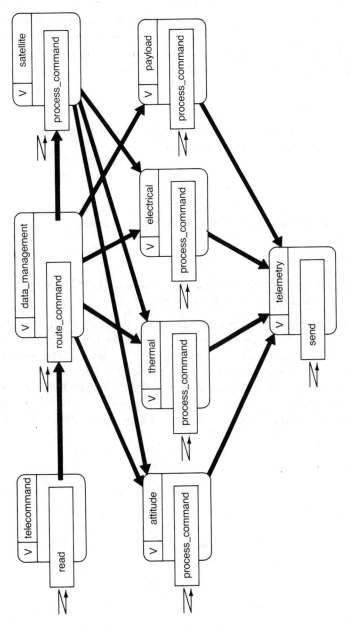

Figure 9.5 Satellite – virtual node objects.

There are enough virtual node objects to allow some flexibility in processor allocation, and so we will accept this as the first draft. These provide not only a functional breakdown of the system, but also the top-level objects by encapsulating the relevant data, and putting the necessary operations in the Provided interface. We may summarise the design method as follows.

APPROACH 1

  1. Produce a HOOD design tree and allocate the objects to the VNs.
  2. Allocate the VNs to processors.

APPROACH 2

  1. Produce a HOOD design tree.
  2. Select each active object at the top level as a VN.

APPROACH 3

  1. For each VN identified above, produce a HOOD design tree.
  2. Allocate the VNs to processors.

The second approach may produce a different result from the other two, since some of the draft VNs above need not be an active object in the top level of the HOOD design tree. In a distributed design, though, a server passive object that is used by several VNs could be more efficiently designed as a VN. An example of this in the satellite design is the telemetry object. This HOOD design is shown in Figure 9.5. Note that several of the VNs have the operation **process_command**, which is a single operation to process all relevant telecommands for that VN.

10

DEVELOPMENTS OF HOOD

HOOD is now being used on several large space, civil and military projects for which Ada is the target programming language. One may foresee certain extensions to the HOOD method, and to the features offered by the supporting CASE tools which will provide extra facilities to the designer and programmer, will add extra target languages, and will extend the use of HOOD into the requirements phase. This does not mean that HOOD is not usable now, nor that HOOD is not stable, since these changes will take place at intervals of about two years. Nor does it mean that older HOOD designs will become obsolete since changes to HOOD will primarily be by extending the method while retaining the current features of HOOD. It is a clear objective of the HOOD User Group to provide upward compatibility from issue to issue, and an objective of the HOOD toolset vendors to provide upward compatibility from tool release to release.

10.1 CASE TOOLS

As HOOD was being defined for the first time, it became apparent that HOOD's adoption by a space project would require the provision of a computer aided software engineering (CASE) tool to support HOOD. The simplest reason for this is that it is difficult to draw and maintain a good HOOD diagram without a specially tailored tool. The second is that it is almost impossible to keep the diagram and ODS of a number of objects consistent with each other without tool support. The most important reason is that, in practice, it is possible to require a standard method to be followed by several hundred people only if there is a CASE tool that both assists the designer in doing so and enforces the method at the same time. In addition, as the customer and prime contractor would have to review all these designs, a standard format was greatly preferred, which would only be achievable by requiring a standard CASE tool.

While HOOD was being developed, the Columbus Manned Space Station project was being defined. The Columbus project team decided to require all software development to be done on a standard Software Development Environment (SDE) consisting of a network of SUN/Unix workstations, so that each software engineer would have good tools to work with. Since Columbus was then the main project for which HOOD was intended, the first HOOD CASE toolset was developed for the Columbus SDE.

The main requirements of a set of HOOD tools are:

1. To support the HOOD method, allowing the design to follow the Basic Design Step for each object, with consistent and standard layouts for each step.
2. To produce standard HOOD documentation from the design data stored in the computer.
3. To check the HOOD rules for each object and between objects, allowing inconsistent states to exist during development, and assisting the designer to resolve inconsistencies.
4. To generate Ada source code and export it to a directory where it can be compiled into an Ada library.
5. To assist in maintaining an object, by allowing the designer to browse through the objects, providing requirement traces and cross-references.
6. To provide editors for each type of HOOD unit, i.e. informal text, structured text and diagrams.
7. To archive and restore HOOD entities, such as an object, a whole HOOD design tree or a subtree.
8. To provide a library for classes and other objects, so that an object can be copied into a design and reused.
9. To support large projects by allowing objects to be imported and exported between computer networks at different sites.

These requirements provide the following benefits:

1. Standardisation of the HOOD method across a large project, and from project to project.
2. Standard documentation produced semi-automatically and tailored to project specific standards, which is important for all readers and reviewers, from customer to subcontractor, from management to quality assurance.
3. Checking of interfaces between objects from an early stage in the design in order to resolve inconsistencies early, and making the interface of an object part of its requirements.
4. Embedding of OBCS and OPCS code sections in automatically generated Ada source that reflects the structure of the design, thus giving automatic

consistency between all Ada source code and the HOOD design to which it corresponds.

5. Access to libraries of objects for reuse within the project, from past projects and in future projects.
6. Improved productivity from reuse of existing objects, from clear designs, from automatic Ada source code generation which keeps consistency between design and code, from ease of change of objects in a CASE tool, from traceability of requirements to specific objects.
7. Good quality diagrams, enabling quick and easy review, which should detect errors earlier, and provide a high-level overview easily.
8. Reuse of designs and objects, giving reuse at a higher level than at the code level (code reuse requires some form of documentation to enable the designer to understand what existing code represents, which is provided by the documentation of a HOOD object).
9. Communication within a large project of designs in computer-readable form, potentially reducing paper volumes and transmission times across a Europe-wide project.

In addition to the traceability provided by the standard HOOD method, a CASE tool that supports another method such as data flow diagrams (DFDs) should provide a trace from a DFD process specification to the OPCS of the corresponding operation that implements the function, and a trace from a data store to the object that implements it, even if these are not one-to-one mappings.

From this list of requirements, we can see an essential list of tools to support HOOD:

Text editor – for informal text units
Diagram editor – for HOOD diagrams
ODS editor – for ODS
HOOD rule checker – to check all formal HOOD rules
Document generator – to generate a set of standard HOOD documents
Ada code generator – to generate Ada source code from the ODS
Library management, archive and export tools

In addition, it may be useful to consider adding some of the following tools and facilities:

Cross-reference Report generator
Reverse engineer – to convert Ada source to a HOOD object
Ada code editor – to edit Ada in the ODS
User interface to the Ada compiler(s)
Quality assurance monitor – an extension of the HOOD rule checker
DFD editor – to support data flow diagrams
Requirements interface and editor

It is important that some of these tools provide a table- or rule-driven interface, so that they can be tailored by the user for each project. By this, it is not intended that a software designer should be able to modify the formats, but that *each project* or part of a project should be able, in a controlled way, to tailor the output formats according to specific needs. Some examples are:

HOOD document generator:

- Provide a set of documents to allow:
  - · a single object
  - · an Architectural Design Document with limited output
  - · a Detailed Design Document with complete output
  - · source code with accompanying HOOD diagrams
- Tailored document front page and page headers and tailers.
- Inclusion of additional external text:
  - · requirements
  - · test plans
  - · quality assurance reports

Ada code generator:

- To provide different formats for:
  - · embedded systems with optimised code (e.g. rename instead of call)
  - · test programs with full trace facilities
  - · simulations with more exception handling and logging
- Different layout and formatting standards.
- Project-specific configuration management data (name, time, date, version).
- To provide additional code generation pragmas.

HOOD rule checker:

- Ability to add or remove rules according to configuration.
- Ability to modify seriousness of rules.

Some users would also appreciate an open interface to the data stored on file (i.e. database) that represents the HOOD design, so that other tools can be made easily. An example might be for more reporting facilities than have been provided by the tool vendor, such as a cross-reference between operations provided and used:

Operation name	Provided by object	Used by object
change	lights	seconds
check	traffic_sensors	seconds

Another example might be the need to change all occurrences of a name or a set of names in the design, e.g. to change **traffic_sensors** to **road_sensors** everywhere it occurs. Without a special interface this will take a significant amount of time for a designer to do item by item. Such a need might well come up after a design review, when significant editorial changes would be needed which are simple to specify but which may require several man-days to perform.

A sample output from a HOOD toolset is included as Appendix E.

10.2 HOOD IN THE SOFTWARE DEVELOPMENT LIFE-CYCLE

10.2.1 Interface to requirements

As a design method, HOOD relies on a good definition of the requirements, without requiring a specific form. While data flow diagrams and state transition diagrams provide a useful start, a more object-oriented requirement definition would be preferable. Object-oriented analysis (OOA) and entity, relationship and attribute (ERA) diagrams provide many additional advantages. The possibility of adding these to the requirements phase to support HOOD is discussed in more detail in section 10.3.1.

Whatever method is used to define the requirements, it is important that the designer should have a good base from which to work. It would be naive to assume that the requirements will be complete, unambiguous and unchanging after the HOOD design begins. Nevertheless, it would be wise to require some measure of completeness and consistency before beginning the design work. This would be achieved by performing a requirements review on a Software Requirements Document, which would be baselined after incorporating changes agreed at the review.

The next step is to provide the requirements in a form that can be mapped into the HOOD objects as the design proceeds. This requires an identifier for each requirement which can be referenced in some way by an object, e.g. by a field in the ODS. It is then possible to provide a mapping and Cross-reference Report of Requirements to Objects and vice versa. For example, using the requirements in Appendix E:

Requirement	Fulfilled by objects
1	traffic_lights
2	traffic_lights
3	traffic_sensors
4	traffic_sensors
5	lights

Object	Fulfils requirements
traffic_lights	1
	2
traffic_sensors	3
	4
lights	5

10.2.2 System configuration

Although HOOD was primarily defined for the design of a single Ada program, HOOD can of course be used to design a set of programs that make up a software system, as well as to design a part of a program as a subcontract. In order to document the idea of a software system, HOOD has the notation of a system configuration, for example:

```
SYSTEM_CONFIGURATION IS
   ROOT OBJECTS
    · root_A, root_B
   CLASSES
      class_X, class_Y
END
```

This means that the system consists of two root objects, **root_A** and **root_B**, which define two programs by their HOOD design trees, and that the two class objects, **class_X** and **class_Y**, are being used to make instance objects somewhere in the HOOD design trees of the root objects.

As we have seen in Chapter 4, section 4.11, an environment object may be used in a HOOD design to represent the Provided interface of an object. Each of the root objects of a system configuration may be seen in this way from an object in the HDT of any other root object. We may show the traffic lights design as a simple example:

```
SYSTEM_CONFIGURATION IS
   ROOT OBJECTS
      traffic_lights
   CLASSES
      lights
END
```

10.2.3 Reuse of objects

While the HOOD Basic Design Step in its simplest form is intended to perform the design process from scratch, it should be extended to consider the possibility of reusing existing objects. This can be done in two ways.

Firstly, as the HOOD design tree is developed, the designer should be aware of objects that already exist in the working environment, as normal active and passive objects. An active or passive object can be incorporated into the design, and reused directly. It may be necessary to copy the object, and then to extend it by adding operations, types or data, etc. It may also be considered necessary to remove some of the features of the object to make the compiled code smaller, although the linker may ignore procedures and functions that are not actually used, in which case it is better for design consistency to retain the redundant operations in the design.

In this way an object may be reused, although if there are significant changes made, a new name, or at least a new version number, should be given to the object. A version number system should be supported by a HOOD tool, possibly by incorporating a formal comment into the ODS for general configuration control purposes.

Secondly, the designer should also be aware of objects that exist in the working environment as class objects. From these class objects, instance objects may be created and used in the design without any further development effort. If the class object has been fully tested, it may not be considered necessary to test the individual instance object further.

10.2.4 Global type package

It is common practice, in developing Ada software where an object-oriented approach is not taken, to provide one or more global packages that contain the types of the software system being designed, possibly partitioned into subgroups in some logical way. This approach does not necessarily lead to the data that are represented by these types being visible, but only the types themselves. The data can remain encapsulated in the packages.

In previous versions of HOOD, this could be done in an object-oriented way by putting these types in the Internals of a parent object, or even the root object, thus providing visibility to the child objects. In *HOOD Reference Manual Issue 3.1.1*, the types can be declared in a parent object as implemented by a type of a child object, where the type is defined fully, thus retaining the definition in the object where it naturally belongs, but providing visibility over a wider area of the design. The child object, ultimately a terminal object, is therefore complete, and, what is more important, it is fully reusable.

Let us look again at the design for the traffic light system. The top-level root object is called **traffic_lights** and we have defined a type **road** as follows:

    TYPE road IS (AC, BD);

This can be used in each object as required. If there had been a child object that was the natural place to define the type **road**, such as an object configuration, then the parent object would have:

    TYPE road IS IMPLEMENTED_BY configuration.road;

This would generate the Ada:

    Subtype road IS configuration.road;

In this way, a type may be defined in the correct object, and may be made visible to a wider set of objects through the Provided interface of a parent object. This process may be repeated up the HOOD design tree, since Ada supports a 'subtype of a subtype'.

10.2.5 Abstract data type model

Some emphasis in Ada design is placed on the concept of an abstract data type, which in HOOD terms may be defined as an object which encapsulates a type and its operations and operators, but without declaring a data item for the type. An example might be shown by a fragment of the ODS:

```
OBJECT adt IS
   . . .
PROVIDED_NTERFACE
   TYPES
      my_type IS private;
   OPERATIONS
      create (x : IN my_type; y : IN string; z : IN integer);
      "+" (x : IN my_type; y : IN my_type) Return my_type;
      print (x : IN my_type);
END_OBJECT adt
```

This would generate the Ada package specification:

```
package adt is
      type my_type is private;
      procedure create (x : IN my_type; y : IN string; z : IN integer);
      function "+" (x : IN my_type; y : IN my_type) Return my_type;
      procedure print (x : IN my_type);
   private
      type my_type is
         record
            name : string (1..30);
            amount : integer;
         end record;
   end adt;
```

The type definition is copied from the ODS Internals into the private part of the specification. The operations are defined in the package body from the OPCS for each operation in the ODS. This object or package may then be used as follows:

```
with adt;
package body USER is
procedure useful is
   a, b, total : adt.my_type;
   begin
      create (a, "Alex", 100);
      create (b, "Edward", 345);
      create (total, "Total", 0);
      total := a + b;
```

```
      print (total);
   end useful;
   end USER;
```

This very simple example of an abstract data type shows how useful it can be because it allows objects **a**, **b** and **total** to be declared with all the operations and operators that are needed. It is very similar to the class construct of C++, without the additional facilities such as inheritance that the C++ class provides.

10.2.6 Prototyping

One of the main uses of the object-oriented programming language Smalltalk is to prototype or simulate a user interface. Smalltalk provides classes to aid in this, and these systems can become operational with the right environment. However, Smalltalk does not provide the right environment for embedded systems, whereas HOOD and Ada are suitable.

HOOD does lend itself to software development by prototyping if by this we mean development by successive refinement, rather than throwaway prototyping. In this sense, we may look at the software development as a succession of steps, where we:

1. Build the overall design structure by developing the full HOOD design tree, thus identifying all the terminal objects, and defining the parent objects that link them together.
2. Refine the main data flows of the program in each ODS to provide a set of operations that will provide an initial functionality.
3. Refine subsidiary data flows in the program, adding successive functions to the system.
4. Refine the error paths to allow full detection and handling of potential errors and to reach full functionality of the system according to the requirements.

Thus we may see the software implementation, i.e. development of full operational code in an incremental way, but putting emphasis in the architectural design phase on a complete structure. Of course, we may expect detailed changes to the design structure as the implementation proceeds, certainly by needing to add operations that have been missed out in the architectural design phase, and possibly even to the extent of needing to add another object. In the worst case, it may be necessary to redesign the structure of the program, with major changes to the parent objects, but if the object orientation of the objects has been done correctly, the major part of the work is preserved in good terminal objects, which can be reconfigured at will with little cost.

10.2.7 Testing

The testing strategy that should be adopted for a HOOD design is similar to that which would be needed for an Ada program of any type. However, HOOD provides good visibility to the structure of the program, and a degree of order so that the testing strategy can easily be defined in terms of objects, using the following guidelines:

- Objects:
  - · An object can be tested through its operations, as a black box.
  - · Objects that are low-level in the seniority hierarchy (servers) can be tested first, then agents can be tested using the servers, and finally actors can be tested, thus completing the seniority hierarchy for a parent containing only terminal objects.
  - · The parent object can be tested next as the sum of its child objects, and so on up the HOOD design tree to the root object.

- Operations:
  - · It may be necessary to test an internal operation by temporarily making it visible as a Provided operation.
  - · Some operations may be able to be tested individually, others will depend on the state of the object being set up by another operation.
  - · The full set of operations needs to be tested together to reflect the state changes of the object.
  - · An operation_set is tested by testing each operation of the set.

- Class objects:
  - · A class object can only be tested as an instance object.
  - · The number of tests required may be limited to the needs of the project, by testing the instance objects needed in the design.
  - · Additional tests covering a wider range of instance objects may be performed to provide a fully validated class object for a class library.

10.2.8 Verification and validation of a HOOD design

The traditional methods of verification and validation apply to a HOOD design, and are supported by the capability of a HOOD toolset to provide formal checking of the HOOD rules which are defined in full in the *HOOD Reference Manual Issue 3.1.1*, Appendix A. These rules provide a complete set as a basis for a HOOD CASE tool, and formalise the descriptions that are given in the manual and in this book.

A HOOD rule may be enforced by the tool structure, e.g. the HOOD diagram can only be produced in certain ways using the shapes provided for an object, and always marking an object with an 'A' for active. A HOOD rule may be enforced by checking an entity online, e.g. that an identifier is a valid Ada identifier, or that only one

Implemented_By link goes from each parent operation. A HOOD rule may also be enforced through offline checks, for example that the entities in the Required interface of one object are in the Provided interface of the corresponding used object.

HOOD also includes some rules, such as the trace of object names through the steps of the HOOD design process, i.e. from the solution strategy to the object identification, then to the object operation table and to the HOOD diagram which may be impossible to check automatically since the solution strategy is probably held as informal text, and the object identification and object operation table may also be informal text. In addition, the name of the object may change from the solution strategy to the HOOD diagram. For example, a solution strategy may use the term 'water pump' whereas the HOOD diagram may call the object more simply 'pump'. There is scope here for a simple database application to provide and maintain this traceability, aided by good documentation of these changes in the object operation table.

In addition, the HOOD Chapter Skeleton is defined in *HOOD Reference Manual Issue 3.1.1*, Appendix D by the definition of the HOOD design process (see also Appendix B of this book). Thus this HOOD 'rule' may be defined by a document generation tool as an outline to be filled in from the HOOD design data for each object.

For the purposes of this section, verification is defined as the verification that the requirements are implemented in the code, and the trace from phase to phase in the software development cycle. Validation is defined as showing that the software meets the needs of the user or customer.

The traditional methods of verification include:

1. Requirements verification, in which the requirements are uniquely identified and traced through the design into the Ada source code. A HOOD object is a design entity that may easily be used for this purpose. One HOOD toolset has extended the Object Description Skeleton with a field for requirement references, so that the requirements fulfilled by the object may be listed, and then cross-reference lists may be produced of requirement–object and object– requirement, and lists of unfulfilled requirements and objects that meet no requirements may be produced. It is not necessarily incorrect to have an object that does not directly fulfil any requirements, since this object may be providing software services at a design solution level, such as a list or table of data. However, it may be useful to check back to the requirements to see if perhaps the requirements should be enhanced or be more explicit in this area.
2. Inspection, in which a team checks the design documentation to see if it is complete and according to standards. At this point, a design checker tool should check that HOOD rules are met, and that the design is complete for the stage reached.
3. Walkthrough, in which the author of a section of design, such as a single object, describes the design with the aid of the HOOD diagram and ODS.

4. Formal review of documentation that is produced according to a standard, marking milestones in the HOOD design process. A formal review should be held at the following points:

- *Architectural design* at the point when the HOOD design tree is completed, and each object has been identified, with all Provided operations and operation_sets. Active objects and constrained operations should be identified. Test plans should exist in outline.
- *Detailed design* at the point when all entries have been made in the Provided interface, Required interface, OBCS and Internals, and the pseudocode has been completed for each OPCS. Test plans should be completed for each object, including parent objects and root object.
- *Code review* at the point where all Ada source code has been written in the OBCS and OPCS CODE sections, and has been compiled and tested at the object level. A code review is needed only for each terminal object.
- *Integration test review* at the point where all objects have been compiled and linked together, and then tested as a whole program. This is equivalent to a full test of the root object. Note that a system of more than one program, in one or more processors will need two levels of integration test.

Validation is achieved by performing tests which correspond to real-life execution of the software in the target hardware or in a realistic simulation of this hardware. HOOD is therefore of little help in the validation tests directly, although HOOD allows the objects that interface this hardware to be identified and debugged independently of the rest of the operational software. The first stage of validation might be achieved in a software simulator, by replacing the hardware interface objects with objects that provide the same operations to the rest of the software, but simulate the effect of the target hardware.

10.2.9 How to review a HOOD design

In addition to the quality assurance aspects covered below, the software engineer who has to review a HOOD design has to answer the following questions:

1. Does the design meet the requirements? This needs an understanding of the requirements, supported by the Cross-reference Reports provided for the design review.
2. Is the design efficient and effective? Will it work? This requires the designer to follow the control flows round the design, ensuring that every operation is used, without any design loops. It is also necessary to trace the interaction between active objects through their constrained operations.
3. Are the objects selected good objects? Each object should encapsulate a good design entity, closely related to the problem being solved.

4. Are exceptions handled properly? Each exception that is raised and propagated should have an appropriate exception handler.
5. Is each active object justified and necessary?

10.2.10 Quality assurance

It is a fundamental tenet that the use of a standard method supported by a CASE tool will improve the quality of the design for any given designer. The designer still has to perform the design work, still has to use experience and understanding of the requirements, and knowledge of how software systems perform to produce a good design, and a good designer may still produce a better design than a bad designer, but both will benefit from a good method and tool. Throughout this book, comments have been made about quality aspects. These are now drawn together.

It is important to say that a good tool will do more than enforce standards, it will actually implement them, since the tools are able to control the output that they produce. Thus we may say that there are four levels at which a tool can assist in improving quality, in descending order of significance:

1. *Implement.* A tool provides the output in a standard way, e.g. a code or document generator.
2. *Enforce.* A tool allows only valid input, e.g. validate an object or operation name as an Ada identifier.
3. *Check.* A tool checks that rules are met, and reports errors, e.g. check that Required interface of a using object matches the Provided interface of the used object.
4. *Enable.* A tool helps the designer to choose a valid option: a tool provides a list of class objects to create an instance object.

We may also identify the following categories.

HOOD rules
The most obvious point is that HOOD provides a set of rules, and that the toolset will check the design against these rules. These are summarised below.

Interface checks
From a design point of view, one important aspect is to check the interfaces between objects early in the design phase, and to maintain these correctly. Ada is very successful in doing this at the code level, but it is well known that the later in the software life-cycle that errors are found, the more expensive it is to correct the errors. Therefore, the concept of checking interfaces even in the architectural design is an important cost reduction factor. This may be performed by a HOOD rule checker.

Requirement Trace and Cross-reference Reports
It is very important for quality assurance to ensure that all requirements are met by
the design. In order to do this, it is preferable that the requirements are allocated to
objects as each object is designed, rather than after the objects have been designed,
thus ensuring that the designer takes the requirements fully into account as the
design work is performed. This can be assisted by providing access to a requirement
database from the HOOD tools, and providing links from each object to each
relevant requirement. These should then be supported by a Cross-reference Report
of Requirements to Objects, and vice versa.

Object completeness
Quality assurance should check that each object has all valid operations. An object
that represents an interface to hardware should have the relevant read or write
operation. An object that represents a piece of data should have at least one
constructor to put data in, and at least one selector to take data out.

Object/Operation Cross-reference Reports
Quality assurance should check these reports to ensure that each Provided operation
is used somewhere in the design, and that each Required operation is provided
somewhere in the design. Discrepancies may occur if an object is reused, but not all
its operations are required for the program.

Architectural Design and Detailed Design Documents
Standard documents are the responsibility of the HOOD document generator tool,
so a quality assurance check is simple.

Data flow names
Since the data flows are an informal selection of the major data flows between
objects, quality assurance must check these individually. Are all major data flows
shown on the HOOD diagram? Are all data flows that are shown on the HOOD
diagram reflected in parameters in the operations in the ODS? (A Cross-reference
Report would be useful here.) Are all data flows shown on the HOOD diagram
sufficiently descriptive or do they conform to a naming or numbering standard?

Justification
The designer should justify each use of an active object or exception. For an active
object, the designer should state that the object is required to be active because:

  1. It handles an interrupt.
  2. It needs its own control flow to constrain at least two operations.
  3. It needs a different priority level from other objects.

Justification of a raised exception should explain the circumstances in which it will be
raised, and the reasons that nothing else can be done. Justification of a handled
exception should explain how it is handled.

Completeness
Quality assurance should check for design completeness of the design at each stage in the life-cycle, according to the standards for that stage. This check is assisted by the HOOD rule checker, and by the relevant document produced by the HOOD document generator, which should have no missing parts.

Ada source code consistency
It is better to modify Ada source code in the HOOD design, using an editor of the ODS, so that the generated Ada source code is always consistent with the CODE section of the ODS stored in the HOOD design. To modify the generated Ada source code outside the HOOD design will lead to a large configuration management problem. In each case, quality assurance should check that the Ada source code is consistent with the HOOD design: for example, check that the entries in the OPCS for operations used and exception propagated are consistent with the Ada source code.

Naming standards
Each tool should provide suitable checks against naming standards, and for valid Ada identifiers.

Coding standards
The coding standards can be implemented by the Ada code generator tool.

DFD checking
When data flow diagrams are used to express the requirements, quality assurance should check the correctness of each DFD, and that each entity in each DFD is mapped into the HOOD design. In particular, a Cross-reference Report should show how each process or function is mapped into one or more operations, how each data store is mapped into one or more objects, how each control process is mapped into an operation, and how each data flow is mapped into a data flow or parameter of an operation.

CORE threads
When CORE is used to express the requirements, a CORE thread is a natural name to express an individual requirement, and may also be used as an operation name in many cases. Quality assurance needs to ensure complete mapping of CORE threads into the design.

10.3 FUTURE EXTENSIONS TO HOOD

10.3.1 Object life-cycle

It is both a strength and a weakness that HOOD makes no preconditions about the method that is used for requirement definition before design with HOOD begins. It is a strength because it means that HOOD can be used in many different environments, where requirements are defined in CORE, Yourdon, SADT or natural language. However, it is a weakness because HOOD has to begin by performing an object-oriented analysis to find the objects for the design. It would be much better if some of this work is done in the requirements phase. Consequently, an object life-cycle is proposed to complete the object-oriented approach to software development.

The essence of an object life-cycle is that much of the effort is spent in analysing, designing and implementing an object, or rather a set of objects. Using this set of objects, with the addition of extra objects purchased as a library, and other objects designed specially to pull them all together, a designer may build an application to meet the needs of a specific project. So the centre of it all is an object. Note that the *object* may in fact be implemented as a *class* in terms of the object-oriented programming language used.

REQUIREMENTS PHASE

The traditional structured methods such as data flow diagrams and SADT, and the data-oriented techniques such as entity relation analysis would be supplemented by object-oriented analysis (OOA) in order to identify and describe the objects which exist in the problem area. Also, whereas the other methods require an application project to be able to be used, OOA can begin by looking in a more abstract way into an application domain, by which we mean the overall set of business or technical entities that we are concerned with. Thus the designer is concerned to identify objects which are fundamental to any computing solutions that may be required in the future.

An object may be found in the same way as described in Chapter 3, by identifying suitable 'things', and then adding to them various lists and descriptions, as follows:

Object Give the name of an object in a free text format.

Attributes
 	
List the attributes of the object.
    · These will become the data and types of the object.
    · Add characteristics of the attribute (type, range, length).

Operations
 	
List the operations that can take place on the object.
    · Describe each operation.
    · Add parameters.

Each attribute and operation can be described more fully as more is learnt about the object. This description can even be written in a formal language if that is appropriate. An object life history may also be defined.

ARCHITECTURAL DESIGN PHASE

These objects can each be designed separately in HOOD, and then implemented, tested, and stored in a library. It is more likely that these object definitions are then incorporated into the requirements for a project, and are fed into the HOOD Basic Design Step. Further objects are then found and a design is produced. The main benefit of using OOA is that many of the objects are already identified, and much of the individual detail is defined at the time when the user is involved, and in a form that the user can understand, rather than being left until the designer is alone with the requirements.

DETAILED DESIGN PHASE

HOOD continues as normal. More effort is made to identify objects that are likely to be reusable, and should perhaps be stored as class object in a class library.

IMPLEMENTATION PHASE

Objects are coded and tested, by refining the OBCS and OPCS CODE sections in the Object Description Skeleton. Selected objects are tested fully with a view to reuse, and the object is fully documented and stored in an object library.

As a result of the object life-cycle, two libraries (an object library and a class library) are produced, providing a strong base for future projects.

10.3.2 Object-oriented language support

HOOD may be adapted to support other languages, especially object-oriented programming languages, such as C++. To do this will involve not only extension of HOOD to include object-oriented analysis in the requirements phase, but also to include an inheritance tree for class objects.

In addition to encapsulation and information hiding, the main features of object-oriented programming languages that are not currently supported by HOOD and Ada are inheritance and polymorphism, which are normally applied to classes rather than objects.

Inheritance is essentially the ability to define a class which is an extension of an existing class (called a base class), so that the new class *inherits* all the attributes (data and types) and all the actions (operations) of the base class. Multiple inheritance is the ability for a class to inherit from more than one base class. The object-oriented programming language Eiffel allows selective inheritance of attributes and actions from multiple base classes. HOOD could therefore be extended to allow a class object to inherit the Provided interface and Internals from one or more other class objects, fully or selectively.

Polymorphism is the ability for the selection of an operation body to be determined at run time, according to the class of the object to which the operation is currently referring. This occurs where there are two or more operations with the same name and parameter list in the class inheritance tree, and when the choice is left open at compile time, for example by using a pointer (access type) in the code to point to an object, the exact nature of which will not be known until run time.

For example, in C++ we may define a simple class inheritance tree for a banking system with classes Account and DepositAccount, and let us assume that each class has an operation called print(). We may then declare a pointer pointAccount to a base class Account, and at run time we may use pointAccount to point to an object A of class Account or an object D of class DepositAccount. This is illustrated with the C++ fragment below:

```
class Account {
public:
    print();
};
class DepositAccount : public Account {
public:
    print();
};
main () {
Account A;
DepositAccount D;
Account *pointAccount;
A.print();
D.print();
pointAccount = &A;
pointAccount -> print();       // uses print() of class Account
pointAccount = &D;
pointAccount -> print();       // uses print() of class DepositAccount
}
```

Overloading is the ability for an operation name to be repeated within a single class definition, providing that there is some way of differentiating between them, by having different parameters (or arguments). Ada and HOOD allow overloading of operations. Ada also allows an operator to be defined for a new type, and also allows an operator to be redefined or overloaded for an existing type, so no changes are needed to HOOD to support overloading.

10.3.3 Additional HOOD features

As part of the evolution of HOOD, some users would like to see features that provide the ability to express all possibilities that are available to the Ada programmer. This can be done in an object oriented context.

Ada provides the capability for a package specification to export a package or a class, so HOOD could be extended to include an object or a class object in the Provided interface of an object. A classic example of this is the package **text_io** which exports the generic package **integer_io**.

HOOD does not allow a task type to appear in the Provided interface, although as is described elsewhere in this book, a task type may be used within an active object. An active class object may also be seen as equivalent to a task type, from which an active instance object is created in a purely static way, i.e. dynamic task generation, is not possible. It would be a valuable extension to the *HOOD Reference Manual* to provide a formal definition of the semantics of HOOD, so that any ambiguity in the current documentation is identified and removed. It would then be possible to provide a validation process for a HOOD CASE toolset. However, this formal definition would require considerable funding, and so is unlikely to happen in the near future.

10.4 STANDARD INTERCHANGE FORMAT

The *HOOD Reference Manual 3.1.1*, Appendix E, defines a Standard Interchange Format (SIF) in order to allow interchange of design data between toolsets and platforms. It may also be used to ease the integration of a HOOD toolset within the Software Development Environment by providing a simple file format for configuration control, analysis by quality assurance tools, etc.

The Object Description Skeleton contains all the necessary design data of each object, except the layout of the HOOD diagram. It was decided that the different HOOD toolsets would not have sufficient compatibility to make it worth defining the HOOD diagram layout as part of the SIF. Consequently, the ODS is the basis of the Standard Interchange Format, supplemented by other textual data stored in the design. This SIF representation will be stored in one or more files containing one or more ODSs according to the choice of the designer and the toolset.

The HOOD toolset will allow as a minimum to exchange:

    The complete design in a HOOD design tree
    One object
    One object and all its descendants

To avoid any potential ambiguity in analysing the ASCII representation of the SIF, the first line of each of the informal text units should start with a specific string called BOT, and the last line should terminate with another string called EOT. The target language dependant parts, such as generated code, should be enclosed between delimiters of BOC and EOC.

The HOOD pragma HCS (see *HOOD Reference Manual Issue 3.1.1*, sections 14.1.1 and 6.10) is used to incorporate text from the informal text in the HOOD chapters into the ODS.

The formal definition of the Standard Interchange Format is based on an ASCII representation of the ODS BNF which is defined in Appendix C of the *HOOD Reference Manual Issue 3.1.1*.

BOT	=	Beginning of Text	=	"--|"
EOT	=	End of Text	=	"|--"
BOC	=	Beginning of Code	=	"--|"
EOC	=	End of Code	=	"|--"

APPENDIX A

HOOD METHOD SUMMARY

A Basic Design Step is split into four phases, thus defining a micro life-cycle for the design of each object. The phases can be summarised as follows:

1. Problem definition.
2. Development of solution strategy.
3. Formalisation of the strategy.
4. Formalisation of the solution.

Each of these phases is described in Chapter 2, section 2.2.

Phase 1. Problem definition

The context of the object to be designed is stated, with the goal of organising and structuring the data from the requirement analysis phase. This is an opportunity to provide a completeness check on requirements and traceability to design.

Subphases:

1.1 Statement of the problem.
1.2 Analysis and structuring of requirement data.

Phase 2. Development of solution strategy

The outline solution of the problem stated above is described in terms of objects at a high level of abstraction.

Phase 3. Formalisation of the strategy

The objects and their associated operations are defined. A HOOD diagram of the proposed design solution is produced, allowing easy visualisation of the concepts and further formalisation.

Subphases:

3.1 Identification of objects (object identification).
3.2 Identification of operations (operation identification).
3.3 Grouping objects and operations (object operation table).
3.4 Graphical description.
3.5 Justification of design decisions.

Phase 4. Formalisation of the solution

The solution is formalised through formal definition of Provided object interfaces and formal description of Object and Operation Control Structures

---

The Basic Design Step is shown as a flowchart in Figure 2.5 on page 15.

APPENDIX B

HOOD CHAPTER SKELETON

HOOD Chapter Skeleton

---

1 Problem definition
   1.1 Problem statement
   1.2 Requirement analysis

2 Informal solution strategy

3 Formalisation of the strategy
   3.1 Object identification
   3.2 Operation identification
   3.3 Object operation table
   3.4 Graphical description
   3.5 Justification of design decisions

4 Formalisation of the solution
   4.1 Object Description Skeleton
   4.2 Generated Ada source code

APPENDIX C

HOOD RESERVED WORDS

The identifiers listed below are HOOD reserved words:

ACTIVE
ASER
ASER_BY_IT
CLASS
CODE
CONSTANTS
CONSTRAINED_BY
CONSTRAINED_OPERATIONS
DATA
DATAFLOWS
DESCRIPTION
END_OBJECT
END_OPERATION
ENVIRONMENT
EXCEPTION_FLOWS
EXCEPTIONS
FORMAL_PARAMETERS
HANDLED_EXCEPTIONS
HSER
HSER_TOER
IMPLEMENTATION_OR_
   SYNCHRONISATION_CONSTRAINTS
IMPLEMENTATION_CONSTRAINTS
IMPLEMENTED_BY
INSTANCE_OF
INSTANCE_RANGE

INTERNALS
LSER
LSER_TOER
MEMBER_OF
NONE
OBJECT
OBJECTS
OBJECT_CONTROL_STRUCTURE
OP_CONTROL
OPERATION
OPERATIONS
OPERATION_CONTROL_
   STRUCTURE
OPERATION_SETS
PARAMETERS
PASSIVE
PROPAGATED_EXCEPTION
PROVIDED_INTERFACE
PSEUDO_CODE
RAISED_BY
REQUIRED_INTERFACE
RETURN
THROUGH
TYPES
USED_OPERATIONS
VIRTUAL_NODE

The identifiers listed below are both HOOD reserved words and Ada reserved words:

IN   OUT
IS   PRAGMA

In addition, the following symbols are used in HOOD:

```
=>
<=
<=>
```

The reserved words are listed in *HOOD Reference Manual Issue 3.1.1*, Appendix B.

APPENDIX D

HEATING SYSTEM REQUIREMENTS

A simple heating system for a house consists of:

1. A timer to control when the heating system will operate.
2. A heater to heat the water.
3. A pump to pump the water around the house.
4. A sensor to measure the temperature of the house.
5. A switch to set the required temperature.

The heating system operates whenever power is supplied to the whole system. Options could allow for:

1. Modification of the water temperature range.
2. Allowing water heating without house heating.

Initialisation

When the heating system is switched on, the timer starts. It checks the actual time against the programmed time to determine when to operate.

Operation

The heater is turned on. When the water temperature reaches 30°C, the pump is switched on. The room temperature is read from the temperature sensor, and when it reaches the required temperature, the pump is switched off. When the water temperature reaches 50°C, the heater is turned off. When the water temperature reaches 30°C, the heater is turned on.

Closedown

There is no closedown action.

APPENDIX **E**

SAMPLE DESIGN: TRAFFIC LIGHTS

TRAFFIC LIGHTS CONTROL SYSTEM
Architectural Design Document

Issue 3.1.1
Date 1 April 1992
Author Peter J. Robinson

CONTENTS

1. Introduction
2. Traffic lights design
   2.1 **traffic_lights**
   2.2 **lights**
   2.3 **seconds**
   2.4 **traffic_sensors**

3. Requirements

4. Cross-reference Tables
   4.1 Requirement Fulfilment Table
   4.2 Objects/Requirements Cross-reference Table
   4.3 Operation/Object Cross-reference Table

1 INTRODUCTION

This document is the architectural design of a simple simulation of a system to control a set of traffic lights. It has been prepared as a demonstration of the HOOD method, and as a sample of a HOOD Architectural Design Document. It is therefore deliberately simple, but it is intended to be complete.

2 TRAFFIC LIGHTS DESIGN

2.1 traffic_lights

2.1.1 PROBLEM DEFINITION

2.1.1.1 *Problem statement*
The traffic lights system controls four traffic lights at a crossroads.
Traffic sensors inform the system of waiting traffic.

2.1.1.2 *Requirement analysis*
All requirements given in Chapter 3 are applicable.

2.1.2 INFORMAL SOLUTION STRATEGY
Initially, the AC lights are set to green, and the BD lights are set to red.

  When the AC lights are green:
After 40 seconds, the BD traffic sensors are checked every second until BD traffic is present,
then the AC lights change to amber, then to red. BD lights change to red-and-amber, then
green.

  When the BD lights are green:
After 20 seconds, the AC traffic sensors and BD traffic sensors are checked every second until
AC traffic is present or BD traffic is not present, then the BD lights change to amber, then red.
AC lights change to red-and-amber, then green.

2.1.3 FORMALISATION OF THE STRATEGY

2.1.3.1 *Object identification*

Objects	Description
seconds	time control every second
AC lights	pair of lights to be changed according to a standard cycle
BD lights	pair of lights to be changed according to a standard cycle
AC traffic sensors	pair of traffic sensors to be checked
BD traffic sensors	pair of traffic sensors to be checked

Objects	Attributes
green	value of light
red	value of light
amber	value of light
red-and-amber	value of light
AC traffic is present	value of AC traffic sensor
BD traffic is present	value of BD traffic sensor
40	value of seconds
20	value of seconds

2.1.3.2 *Operation identification*

Operations
_____

check
change
count   implied for seconds

2.1.3.3 *Object operation table*

Objects	Operation
seconds	count
AC lights	change
BD lights	change
AC traffic sensors	check
BD traffic sensors	check

This table can be generalised by combining AC and BD objects as follows:

Objects	Operation
seconds	count
lights	change
traffic sensors	check

2.1.3.4 *Graphical description*
See Figure E.1.

2.1.3.5 *Justification of design decisions*
The root object **traffic lights** is an active object since there is a 1 Hz clock interrupt.

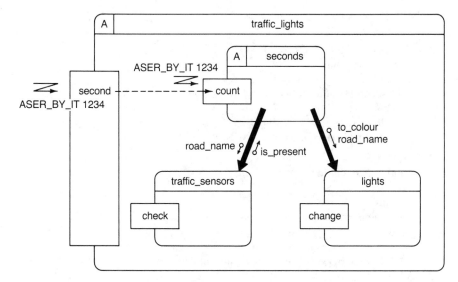

Figure E.1 HOOD diagram of **traffic_lights.**

2.1.4 FORMALISATION OF THE SOLUTION

2.1.4.1 *Object Description Skeleton*

    OBJECT traffic_lights IS ACTIVE
        PRAGMA TARGET_LANGUAGE Ada

    DESCRIPTION
        The traffic lights system controls four traffic lights at a crossroads. The traffic
        sensors inform the system of waiting traffic.

    IMPLEMENTATION_CONSTRAINTS
        The system is driven by a 1 Hz clock.

    PROVIDED_INTERFACE
     TYPES
       NONE
     CONSTANTS
       NONE
     OPERATION_SETS
       NONE
     OPERATIONS
       second;
     EXCEPTIONS
       NONE

    REQUIRED_INTERFACE
       NONE

    DATAFLOWS
       NONE

    EXCEPTION_FLOWS
       NONE

    OBJECT_CONTROL_STRUCTURE
       -- obcs_synchronisation
     DESCRIPTION
       Each second, traffic_lights is activated to look at the traffic sensors and to change
       the lights.
     CONSTRAINED_OPERATIONS
       second CONSTRAINED_BY ASER_BY_IT#1234;

    INTERNALS
       -- internal_definitions
     OBJECTS
       seconds;
       traffic_sensors;
       lights;
     TYPES
       road IS (AC, BD);   --| defines road configuration |--
     DATA
       NONE

```
      CONSTANTS
        NONE
      OPERATION_SETS
        NONE
      OPERATIONS
        second IMPLEMENTED_BY seconds.count;
      EXCEPTIONS
        NONE

    OBJECT_CONTROL_STRUCTURE
      -- obcs_implementation
    IMPLEMENTED_BY
      seconds;

    END_OBJECT traffic_lights
```

2.1.4.2 *Generated Ada source code*

```
    --H Generated Ada source code of traffic_lights
    --H main procedure of the program
    --H    calls unconstrained operations of root object (if any),
    --H    constrained operations of root object are interrupt driven
    --H
    with traffic_lights;
    procedure traffic_lights_main is
    begin
      null;                        -- program is interrupt driven
    end traffic_lights_main;

    --H package specification
    --H
    with seconds;
    package traffic_lights is
      type road IS (AC, BD);       --| defines road configuration |--
    --H procedure second is not needed, since child operation is
    --H interrupt driven
    end traffic_lights;
```

2.2 lights

2.2.1 PROBLEM DEFINITION

2.2.1.1 *Problem statement*

Object **lights** is used to set a traffic light pair to a selected colour, allowing for proper sequencing of all lights as necessary for safety.

2.2.1.2 *Requirement analysis*

Requirements applicable are:

R08. The traffic lights are changed in the cycle from green to amber to red, and from red to red-and-amber to green.

2.2.2 INFORMAL SOLUTION STRATEGY

The data item **other_road** is initialised to the opposite of the value of **road_ name.**

   If the requested colour is green, operation change controls the full sequencing from green to amber to red for one light set, and red to red-and-amber to green for the other light set.

   If the requested colour is red or amber, operation change simply sets the requested light to red or amber.

2.2.3 FORMALISATION OF THE STRATEGY

2.2.3.1 *Object identification*

Object	Description/attribute
other_road	attribute
road_name	attribute
colour	attribute
GREEN	value of colour
AMBER	value of colour
RED	value of colour
RED_AMBER	value of colour

2.2.3.2 *Operation identification*

Operations
initialise

2.2.3.3 *Object operation table*
No new objects, so this is a terminal object.

2.2.3.4 *Graphical description*
See Figure E.2.

2.2.3.5 *Justification of design decisions*
None.

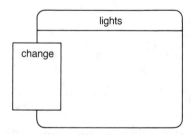

Figure E.2 HOOD diagram of **lights**.

2.2.4 FORMALISATION OF THE SOLUTION

2.2.4.1 *Object Description Skeleton*

    OBJECT lights IS PASSIVE
        PRAGMA TARGET_LANGUAGE Ada

    DESCRIPTION
        Object lights is used to set a traffic light pair to a selected colour, allowing for
        proper sequencing of all lights as necessary for safety.

    IMPLEMENTATION_CONSTRAINTS
        In this simulation, text_io is used to provide a readable output.

    PROVIDED_INTERFACE
        -- provided_interface_definitions
        TYPES
        colour IS (red, red_amber, green, amber);
        CONSTANTS
            NONE
        OPERATION_SETS
            NONE
        OPERATIONS
            change (road_name : IN traffic_lights.road;
                    to_colour : IN colour);
        EXCEPTIONS
            NONE

    REQUIRED_INTERFACE
        -- required_interface_definitions

    OBJECT traffic_lights;
        TYPES
        road;   --| defined in parent object as needed throughout |--
        CONSTANTS
            NONE
        OPERATION_SETS
            NONE
        OPERATIONS
            NONE
        EXCEPTIONS
            NONE

    OBJECT text_io;
        TYPES
            NONE
        CONSTANTS
            NONE
        OPERATION_SETS
            NONE
        OPERATIONS
            put_line (item : IN string);   --| print a string |--

EXCEPTIONS
  NONE

DATAFLOWS
  NONE

EXCEPTION_FLOWS
  NONE

INTERNALS
  -- internal_definitions
  OBJECTS
    NONE
  TYPES
    NONE
  DATA
    other_road : traffic_lights.road;   --| no initial value |--
  CONSTANTS
    NONE
  OPERATION_SETS
    NONE
  OPERATIONS
    NONE
  EXCEPTIONS
    NONE

OPERATION_CONTROL_STRUCTURES

OPERATION change (road_name : IN traffic_lights.road;
                          to_colour : IN colour)
  DESCRIPTION
    The data item other_road is initialised to the opposite of the value of road_name.
    If the requested colour is GREEN, operation change controls the full sequencing
    from GREEN to AMBER to RED for one light set, and RED to RED_AMBER
    to GREEN for the other light set.
    If the requested colour is RED or AMBER, operation change simply sets the
    requested light to RED or AMBER.

  USED_OPERATIONS
    text_io.put_line;
  PROPAGATED_EXCEPTIONS
    NONE
  HANDLED_EXCEPTIONS
    NONE
  PSEUDO_CODE
    if road_name = AC then
        set other_road = BD
    else
        set other_road = AC
    end if
    if to_colour = green then

```
                set other_road to amber
                set road_name to red_amber
                set other_road to red
                set road_name to green
            else
                set road_name to to_colour
            end if
        CODE
            use traffic_light;        -- for equality operator of type road
            begin
            if road_name = traffic_lights.AC then
                other_road := traffic_lights.BD;
            else
                other_road := traffic_lights.AC;
            end if;
            if to_colour = green then
                text_io.put_line ("Setting " &
                    traffic_lights.road'image(other_road) & " to amber");
                text_io.put_line ("Setting " &
                    traffic_lights.road'image(road_name) & " to red_amber");
                text_io.put_line ("Setting " &
                    traffic_lights.road'image(other_road) & " to red");
                text_io.put_line ("Setting " &
                    traffic_lights.road'image(road_name) & " to green");
            else
                text_io.put_line ("Setting " &
                    traffic_lights.road'image(road_name) & " to " &
                        colour'image(to_colour));
            end if;
        END_OPERATION change

    END_OBJECT lights
```

2.2.4.2 *Generated Ada source code*

```
--H Generated Ada source code of lights
--H package specification
with traffic_lights;
package lights is
    type colour IS (red, red_amber, green, amber);
    procedure change (road_name : IN traffic_lights.road;
                      to_colour : IN colour);
end lights;

--H package body
with text_io;
package body lights is
    other_road : traffic_lights.road;        --| no initial value |--
```

```
procedure change (road_name : IN traffic_lights.road;
                       to_colour : IN colour) is
--H
--H if road_name = AC then
--H     set other_road = BD
--H else
--H     set other_road = AC
--H end if
--H if to_colour = green then
--H     set other_road to amber
--H     set road_name to red_amber
--H     set other_road to red
--H     set road_name to green
--H else
--H     set road_name to to_colour
--H end if
--H
use traffic_light;      -- for equality operator of type road
begin
    if road_name = traffic_lights.AC then
        other_road := traffic_lights.BD;
    else
        other_road := traffic_lights.AC;
    end if;
    if to_colour = green then
        text_io.put_line ("Setting " &
            traffic_lights.road'image(other_road) & " to amber");
        text_io.put_line ("Setting " &
            traffic_lights.road'image(road_name) & " to red_amber");
        text_io.put_line ("Setting " &
            traffic_lights.road'image(other_road) & " to red");
        text_io.put_line ("Setting " &
            traffic_lights.road'image(road_name) & " to green");
    else
        text_io.put_line ("Setting " &
            traffic_lights.road'image(road_name) & " to " &
                colour'image(to_colour) );
    end if;
end change;
end lights;
```

2.3 seconds

2.3.1 PROBLEM DEFINITION

2.3.1.1 *Problem statement*
The object **seconds** is driven by a clock interrupt to control the traffic lights.

2.3.1.2 *Requirement analysis*

R02. Initially, the AC lights are set to green, and the BD lights are set to red.

R04. The main road AC is given 40 seconds of green lights each cycle.

R05. If there is traffic waiting for BD, then the side roads BD are given 20 seconds of green each cycle.

R06. If there is traffic waiting in only one direction, the lights stay green in that direction.

R07. If there is no traffic waiting, the main road AC is green.

R09. Time is obtained from a 1 Hz clock interrupt.

2.3.2 INFORMAL SOLUTION STRATEGY

Object **seconds** is activated from its parent object **traffic_lights** by the operation **traffic_lights.second**. It checks for traffic and changes the lights if appropriate.

Seconds keeps count of the time since the last light change and the road pair that is green (AC/BD).

After 40/20 seconds have elapsed, **seconds** checks the traffic sensors each second. When the traffic sensors show that there is traffic waiting at the other road, the lights are changed.

2.3.3 FORMALISATION OF THE STRATEGY

2.3.3.1 *Object identification*

Object	Description/attribute
seconds	This object
traffic	External entity
lights	Used Object
time	External entity
road pair	External entity
green	value of colour attribute of lights
traffic sensors	Used Object

2.3.3.2 *Operation identification*

Operations	Description
activated	operation of seconds
checks	operation of traffic sensors
changes	operation of lights
keeps a count	internal action

2.3.3.3 *Object operation table*

No new objects, so this is a terminal object.

2.3.3.4 *Graphical description*

See Figure E.3.

2.3.3.5 *Justification of design decisions*

Seconds is an active object driven by a 1 Hz interrupt at address 1234 through its constrained operation count.

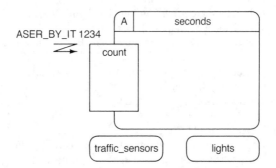

Figure E.3 HOOD diagram of **seconds**.

2.3.4 FORMALISATION OF THE SOLUTION

2.3.4.1 *Object Description Skeleton*

OBJECT seconds IS ACTIVE
    PRAGMA TARGET_LANGUAGE Ada

DESCRIPTION
    Object seconds is activated from its parent object traffic_lights by the operation
    traffic_lights.second. It checks for traffic and changes the lights if appropriate.
    Seconds keeps a count of the time since the last light change and the road pair that
    is green (AC/BD).
    After 40/20 seconds elapsed, seconds checks the traffic_sensors each second. When
    the traffic sensors show that there is traffic waiting at the other road, the lights are
    changed.

IMPLEMENTATION_OR_SYNCHRONISATION_CONSTRAINTS
    Operation count of object seconds is activated once every second by interrupt at
    address 1234.

PROVIDED_INTERFACE
    -- provided_interface_definitions
    TYPES
        NONE
    CONSTANTS
        NONE
    OPERATION_SETS
        NONE
    OPERATIONS
        count;   --| activated by interrupt |--
    EXCEPTIONS
        NONE

REQUIRED_INTERFACE
    -- required_interface_definitions

```
OBJECT traffic_lights;
  TYPES
    road;      --| defined in parent object as needed throughout |--
  CONSTANTS
    NONE
  OPERATION_SETS
    NONE
  OPERATIONS
    NONE
  EXCEPTIONS
    NONE

OBJECT lights;
  TYPES
    colour;
  CONSTANTS
    NONE
  OPERATION_SETS
    NONE
  OPERATIONS
    change;
  EXCEPTIONS
    NONE

OBJECT traffic_sensors;
  TYPES
    present;
  CONSTANTS
    NONE
  OPERATION_SETS
    NONE
  OPERATIONS
    check;
  EXCEPTIONS
    NONE

DATAFLOWS
    road_name => lights;
    to_colour => lights;
    road_name => traffic_sensors;
    is_present <= traffic_sensors;

EXCEPTION_FLOWS
    NONE

OBJECT_CONTROL_STRUCTURE
    -- obcs_synchronisation
  DESCRIPTION
    Seconds keeps a count of the time since the last light change, and the road pair that
    is green (AC/BD).
    After 40/20 seconds elapsed, control checks the traffic_sensors each second.
```

CONSTRAINED_OPERATIONS
count CONSTRAINED_BY ASER_BY_IT#1234;

INTERNALS
-- internal_definitions
OBJECTS
NONE
TYPES
second IS new integer;
DATA
elapsed : second := 0;
ac_present : traffic_sensors.present;
bd_present : traffic_sensors.present;
current_green_pair : traffic_lights.road := traffic_lights.AC;
CONSTANTS
NONE
OPERATION_SETS
NONE
OPERATIONS
NONE
EXCEPTIONS
NONE

OBJECT_CONTROL_STRUCTURE
-- obcs_implementation

PSEUDO_CODE
loop
    select
        accept COUNT and call its OPCS
    end select;
end loop;

CODE
loop
    select
        accept COUNT do
            OPCS_COUNT;
        end COUNT;
    end select;
end loop;

OPERATION_CONTROL_STRUCTURES
-- operation_definitions for terminal objects

OPERATION count
DESCRIPTION
This operation implements the logic of operation seconds to control traffic light changes according to the presence of traffic on the two road pairs.
USED_OPERATIONS
lights.change;

```
        traffic_sensors.check;
PROPAGATED_EXCEPTIONS
    NONE
HANDLED_EXCEPTIONS
    NONE
PSEUDO_CODE
    loop
        count time since last lights change
        if delay has reached (40 for AC) | (20 for BD) then
            check the other road for traffic present
            for AC : if BD traffic present then
                    set AC lights to red, BD lights to green
            for BD : if AC traffic present or no BD traffic then
                    set BD lights to red, AC lights to green
            reset time count
    end loop

CODE
    use traffic_light;        -- for equality operator of type road
    begin
    elapsed := elapsed + 1;
    if current_green_pair = traffic_lights.AC then
        if elapsed >= 40 then
            traffic_sensors.check (traffic_lights.BD, bd_present);
            if bd_present = true then
                lights.change (traffic_lights.BD, lights.green);
                current_green_pair := traffic_lights.BD;
                elapsed := 0;
            end if;
        end if;
    else       -- current_green_pair = BD
        if elapsed >= 20 then
            traffic_sensors.check (traffic_lights.BD, bd_present);
            traffic_sensors.check (traffic_lights.AC, ac_present);
            if ac_present = true or bd_present = false then
                lights.change (traffic_lights.AC, lights.green);
                current_green_pair := traffic_lights.AC;
                elapsed := 0;
            end if;
        end if;
    end if;
    END_OPERATION count

END OBJECT seconds
```

2.3.4.2 *Generated Ada source code*

--H Generated Ada source code of seconds

--H package specification

```
package seconds is
    procedure count;
end seconds;

--H package seconds body
with traffic_lights;
with lights;
with traffic_sensors;
package body seconds is

--H TYPES
    type second IS new integer;

--H DATA
    elapsed : second := 0;
    ac_present : traffic_sensors.present;
    bd_present : traffic_sensors.present;
    current_green_pair : traffic_lights.road := traffic_lights.AC

--H OBCS specification
--H
task OBCS is
    entry count;
        for count use at 1234;
end OBCS;

--H operation renames entry point in task OBCS
--H
procedure count renames OBCS.count;

procedure OPCS_COUNT;        -- forward declaration required
--H OBCS body
task body OBCS is
--H PSEUDO_CODE
--H loop
--H    select
--H        accept COUNT and call its OPCS
--H    end select;
--H end loop;
--H
begin
    loop
        select
            accept COUNT do
                OPCS_COUNT;
            end COUNT;
        end select;
    end loop;
end OBCS;

procedure OPCS_count is
```

```
--H PSEUDO_CODE
--H loop
--H     count time since last lights change
--H     if delay has reached (40 for AC) | (20 for BD) then
--H         check the other road for traffic present
--H         for AC : if BD traffic present then
--H             set AC lights to red, BD lights to green
--H         for BD : if AC traffic present or no BD traffic then
--H             set BD lights to red, AC lights to green
--H         reset time count
--H end loop
--H
use traffic_light;        -- for equality operator of type road
begin
    elapsed := elapsed + 1;
    if current_green_pair = traffic_lights.AC then
        if elapsed >= 40 then
            traffic_sensors.check (traffic_lights.BD, bd_present);
            if bd_present = true then
                lights.change (traffic_lights.BD, lights.green);
                current_green_pair := traffic_lights.BD;
                elapsed := 0;
            end if;
        end if;
    else      -- current_green_pair = BD
        if elapsed >= 20 then
            traffic_sensors.check (traffic_lights.BD, bd_present);
            traffic_sensors.check (traffic_lights.AC, ac_present);
            if ac_present = true or bd_present - false then
                lights.change (traffic_lights.AC, lights.green;
                current_green_pair := traffic_lights.AC;
                elapsed := 0;
            end if;
        end if;
    end if;
end OPCS_count;

end seconds;
```

2.4 traffic_sensors

2.4.1 PROBLEM DEFINITION

2.4.1.1 *Problem statement*
The object **traffic_sensors** checks the traffic sensors.

2.4.1.2 *Requirement analysis*

R03. Traffic sensors are checked to inform the system of waiting traffic.

2.4.2 INFORMAL SOLUTION STRATEGY
See above.

2.4.3 FORMALISATION OF THE STRATEGY

2.4.3.1 *Object identification*

Object	Description/attribute
traffic_sensors	this object
traffic	external trigger for traffic_sensors

2.4.3.2 Operation identification

Operations
check

2.4.3.3 *Object operation table*
No new objects, so this is a terminal object.

2.4.3.4 *Graphical description*
See Figure E.4.

2.4.3.5 *Justification of design decisions*
None.

2.4.4 FORMALISATION OF THE SOLUTION

2.4.4.1 *Object Description Skeleton*

OBJECT traffic_sensors IS PASSIVE
    PRAGMA TARGET_LANGUAGE Ada

DESCRIPTION
    Object traffic_sensors reads the hardware sensor data to find out if traffic is present, and returns the value is_present set to TRUE or FALSE.

IMPLEMENTATION_OR_SYNCHRONISATION_CONSTRAINTS
    NONE

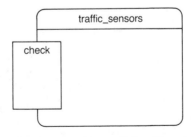

Figure E.4 HOOD diagram of **traffic_sensors**.

PROVIDED_INTERFACE
    -- provided_interface_definitions
  TYPES
    present IS BOOLEAN;   --| TRUE if traffic is present |--
  CONSTANTS
    NONE
  OPERATION_SETS
    NONE
  OPERATIONS
    check (road_name : IN traffic_lights.road;
         is_present : IN OUT present);
  EXCEPTIONS
    NONE

REQUIRED_INTERFACE
    -- required_interface_definitions

OBJECT traffic_lights;
  TYPES
    road;   --| defined in parent object as needed throughout |--
  CONSTANTS
    NONE
  OPERATION_SETS
    NONE
  OPERATIONS
    NONE
  EXCEPTIONS
    NONE

DATAFLOWS
    NONE

EXCEPTION_FLOWS
    NONE

INTERNALS
    -- internal_definitions
  OBJECTS
    NONE
  TYPES
    address is range 1..4;
  DATA
    ac_sensors : array (1..2) of address := (1, 2);
    bd_sensors : array (1..2) of address := (3, 4);
  CONSTANTS
    NONE
  OPERATION_SETS
    NONE
  OPERATIONS
    read_sensor (sensor_address : IN address) RETURN present;

EXCEPTIONS
NONE

OPERATION_CONTROL_STRUCTURES
-- operation_definitions for terminal objects

OPERATION check (road_name : IN traffic_lights.road;
                          is present : IN OUT present)
DESCRIPTION
Operation check reads the hardware sensors for the road given in the parameter
road_name to find out if traffic is present on either side, and returns the value
is_present set to TRUE or FALSE.
USED_OPERATIONS
NONE
PROPAGATED_EXCEPTIONS
NONE
HANDLED_EXCEPTIONS
NONE
PSEUDO_CODE
for each traffic sensor in road loop
    read traffic sensor (address)
    set returned value in is_present
    exit when is_present
end loop;

CODE
i : integer;
use traffic_light;   -- for equality operator of type road
begin
if road_name = traffic_lights.AC then
    for i in ac_sensors'range loop
        is_present := read_sensor (ac_sensors (i));
        exit when is_present;
    end loop;
else   -- road_name = BD
    for i in bd_sensors'range loop
        is_present := read_sensor (bd_sensors (i));
        exit when is_present;
    end loop;
end if;
end;
END_OPERATION check

OPERATION read_sensor (sensor_address : IN address) RETURN present
DESCRIPTION
Operation read_sensor reads a hardware sensor at the given sensor address, and
returns the value TRUE or FALSE.
USED_OPERATIONS
NONE

```
PROPAGATED_EXCEPTIONS
   NONE
HANDLED_EXCEPTIONS
   NONE
PSEUDO_CODE
   For this simulation, always return the value TRUE.
CODE
   return TRUE;
END_OPERATION read_sensor
```

END_OBJECT traffic_sensor

2.4.4.2 *Generated Ada source code*

```
--H Generated Ada source code of traffic_sensor
with traffic_lights;
package traffic_sensors is
    subtype present is boolean;
    --| TRUE if traffic is present --|
    procedure check (road_name : in traffic_lights.road;
                     is_present : in out present);
end traffic_sensors;

package body traffic_sensors is
type address is range 1..4;
ac_sensors : array (1..2) of address := (1, 2);
bd_sensors : array (1..2) of address := (3, 4);

function read_sensor (sensor_address : IN address) RETURN present is
--H For this simulation, always return the value TRUE.
--H
begin
    return TRUE;
end read_sensor;

procedure check (road_name : IN traffic_lights.road;
                 is_present : IN OUT present) is
--H for each traffic sensor in road loop
--H    read traffic sensor (address)
--H    set returned value in is_present
--H    exit when is_present
--H end loop;
--H
i : integer;
use traffic_light;      -- for equality operator of type road
begin
    if road_name = traffic_lights.AC then
        for i in ac_sensors'range loop
            is present := read_sensor (ac_sensors (i));
            exit when is_present;
```

```
        end loop;
    else      -- road_name = BD
        for i in bd_sensors'range loop
            is_present := read_sensor (bd_sensors (i));
            exit when is_present;
        end loop;
    end if;
end check;
end traffic_sensors;
```

3 REQUIREMENTS

R01. The traffic lights system controls four traffic lights at a crossroads where road AC crosses road BD.

R02. Initially, the AC lights are set to green, and the BD lights are set to red.

R03. Traffic sensors are checked to inform the system of waiting traffic.

R04. The main road AC is given 40 seconds of green lights each cycle.

R05. If there is traffic waiting for BD, then the side roads BD are given 20 seconds of green each cycle.

R06. If there is traffic waiting in only one direction, the lights stay green in that direction.

R07. If there is no traffic waiting, the main road AC is green.

R08. The traffic lights are changed in the cycle from green to amber to red, and from red to red-and-amber to green.

R09. Time is obtained from a 1 Hz clock interrupt.

4 CROSS-REFERENCE TABLES

4.1 Requirement Fulfilment Table

Requirement	Object
R01	traffic_lights
R02	traffic_lights
	seconds
R03	traffic_lights
	traffic_sensors
R04	traffic_lights
	seconds
R05	traffic_lights
	seconds
R06	traffic_lights
	seconds

R07	traffic_lights
	seconds
R08	traffic_lights
	lights
R09	traffic_lights
	seconds

4.2 Objects/Requirements Cross-reference Table

Object	Requirements
traffic_lights	R01 R02 R03 R04 R05 R06 R07 R08 R09
lights	R08
seconds	R02 R04 R05 R06 R07 R09
traffic_sensors	R03

4.3 Operation/Object Cross-reference Table

Operation	Object
change	lights
check	traffic_sensors
count	seconds
second	traffic_lights

APPENDIX F

ODS OF CLASS OBJECT lights AND INSTANCE OBJECT lights_ac

1 ODS OF CLASS OBJECT lights

An alternative approach to the design of the traffic lights system in Appendix E is to develop a class object **lights** and then to make two instance objects called **lights_ac** and **lights_bd** to put in the HOOD design tree. This appendix contains the Object Description Skeleton of class object **lights** and instance object **lights_ac**, followed by the corresponding generated Ada source code.

```
OBJECT lights IS CLASS PASSIVE
   FORMAL_PARAMETERS
      TYPES
         t_road;                    --| defines possible light sets |--
      CONSTANTS
         road_name : t_road;        --| value of type road |--
      OPERATION_SETS
         NONE
      OPERATIONS
         set_other_road (x : IN t_road);
                                    --| set value of other road |--
      PRAGMA TARGET_LANGUAGE Ada

DESCRIPTION
   Object lights is used to set a traffic light pair to a selected colour, allowing for
   proper sequencing of all lights as necessary for safety.

IMPLEMENTATION_OR_SYNCHRONISATION_CONSTRAINTS
   In this simulation, text_io is used to provide a readable output.

PROVIDED_INTERFACE
   -- provided_interface_definitions
   TYPES
      Type colour IS (red, red_amber, green, amber);
```

```
      CONSTANTS
        NONE
      OPERATION_SETS
        NONE
      OPERATIONS
        change (to_colour : IN colour);
      EXCEPTIONS
        NONE

REQUIRED_INTERFACE
      -- required_interface_definitions

OBJECT text_io;
    TYPES
      NONE
    CONSTANTS
      NONE
    OPERATION_SETS
      NONE
    OPERATIONS
      put_line (item : IN string);        --| print a string |--
    EXCEPTIONS
      NONE
DATAFLOWS
    NONE

EXCEPTION_FLOWS
    NONE

INTERNALS
    -- internal_definitions
    OBJECTS
      NONE
    TYPES
      NONE
    DATA
      other_road : t_road;         --| initial value not necessary |--
    CONSTANTS
      NONE
    OPERATION_SETS
      NONE
    OPERATIONS
      NONE
    EXCEPTIONS
      NONE

OPERATION_CONTROL_STRUCTURES

OPERATION change (to_colour : IN colour)
    DESCRIPTION
```

The data item other_road is initialised to the opposite of the value of road_name.
If the requested colour is GREEN, operation change controls the full sequencing
from GREEN to AMBER to RED for one light set, and RED to RED_AMBER
to GREEN for the other light set.

If the requested colour is RED or AMBER, operation change simply sets the
requested light to RED or AMBER.

USED_OPERATIONS
    text_io.put_line; ·
PROPAGATED_EXCEPTIONS
    NONE
HANDLED_EXCEPTIONS
    NONE
PSEUDO_CODE
    set other_road with Formal Parameter operation
    if to_colour = green then
        set other_road to amber
        set road_name to red_amber
        set other_road to red
        set road_name to green
    else
        set road_name to to_colour
    end if

CODE
    set_other_road (other_road);
    if to_colour = green then
        text_io.put_line
            ("Setting " & t_road'image(other_road) & " to amber");
        text_io.put_line
            ("Setting " & t_road'image(road_name) & " to red_amber");
        text_io.put_line
            ("Setting " & t_road'image(other_road) & " to red");
        text_io.put_line
            ("Setting " & t_road'image(road_name) & " to green");
    else
        text_io.put_line
            ("Setting " & t_road'image(road_name) & " to "
                & colour'image(to_colour));
    end if;
    END_OPERATION change

END_OBJECT lights

--H Generated Ada source code of Class Object lights

--H package specification
with traffic_lights;
with text_io;
generic

```
      type t_road is (<>);
      road_name : t_road;
      procedure set_other_road (x : IN t_road);

package lights is
      Type colour IS (red, red_amber, green, amber);
      procedure change (to_colour : IN colour);
end lights;

--H package body
package body lights is
      other_road : t_road;      --| initial value not necessary |--
procedure change (to_colour : IN colour) is
--H
--H set other_road with Formal Parameter operation
--H if to_colour = green then
--H     set other_road to amber
--H     set road_name to red_amber
--H     set other_road to red
--H     set road_name to green
--H else
--H     set road_name to to_colour
--H end if
--H
begin
    set_other_road (other_road);
    if to_colour = green then
        text_io.put_line
            ("Setting " & t_road'image(other_road) & " to amber");
        text_io.put_line
            ("Setting " & t_road'image(road_name) & " to red_amber");
        text_io.put_line
            ("Setting " & t_road'image(other_road) & " to red");
        text_io.put_line
            ("Setting " & t_road'image(road_name) & " to green");
    else
        text_io.put_line
            ("Setting " & t_road'image(road_name & " to "
                & colour'image(to_colour)));
    end if;
end change;

end lights;
```

2 ODS OF INSTANCE OBJECT lights_ac

OBJECT lights_ac IS INSTANCE_OF lights
  PARAMETERS
    TYPES
      t_road => road_pair;
    CONSTANTS
      road_name => AC;
    OPERATION_SETS
      NONE
    OPERATIONS
      set_other_road => set_other_road_bd;
    PRAGMA TARGET_LANGUAGE Ada

DESCRIPTION
  Object lights is used to set a traffic light pair to a selected colour, allowing for proper sequencing of all lights as necessary for safety.

IMPLEMENTATION_OR_SYNCHRONISATION_CONSTRAINTS
  In this simulation, text_io is used to provide a readable output.

PROVIDED_INTERFACE
  – provided_interface_definitions
  TYPES
    Type colour IS (red, red_amber, green, amber);
  CONSTANTS
    NONE
  OPERATION_SETS
    NONE
  OPERATIONS
    change (to_colour : IN colour);
  EXCEPTIONS
    NONE

REQUIRED_INTERFACE
  -- required_interface_definitions

OBJECT text_io;
  TYPES
    NONE
  CONSTANTS
    NONE
  OPERATION_SETS
    NONE
  OPERATIONS
    put_line (item :IN string);   --| print a string |--
  EXCEPTIONS
    NONE

DATAFLOWS
    NONE

EXCEPTION_FLOWS
    NONE

END_OBJECT lights_ac

--H Generated Ada source code of Intance Object lights_ac
package lights_ac is new lights (road_pair, AC, set_other_road_bd);

Note that the type **road_pair** and the procedure **set_other_road_bd** must be defined and be made visible to this package instantiation.

APPENDIX **G**

ODS OF ACTIVE OBJECTS
FIFO_Queue *AND* **Interrupt**

1 ODS OF ACTIVE OBJECT FIFO_Queue

OBJECT FIFO_Queue IS ACTIVE
    PRAGMA TARGET_LANGUAGE Ada

DESCRIPTION
    This object maintains a FIFO Queue of buffer data from the interrupts. Data are stored in the queue using operation add_entry. Data may be read for processing using operation remove_entry

IMPLEMENTATION_OR_SYNCHRONISATION_CONSTRAINTS
    The operations are constrained so that only one may be processing at a time.
    Data may not be added when the queue is full.
    Data may not be removed when the queue is empty.

PROVIDED_INTERFACE
    -- provided_interface_definitions
  TYPES
    value IS private;
  CONSTANTS
    NONE
  OPERATION_SETS
    NONE
  OPERATIONS
    add_entry (x : IN value);
    remove_entry (x : OUT value);
  EXCEPTIONS
    NONE

REQUIRED_INTERFACE
    NONE

DATAFLOWS
  NONE

EXCEPTION_FLOWS
  NONE

OBJECT_CONTROL_STRUCTURE
  -- obcs_synchronisation
  DESCRIPTION
  The OBCS constrains the operations to be mutually exclusive. Operation add_
  entry is Loosely Synchronous so as not to delay the Interrupt Handler.
  CONSTRAINED_OPERATIONS
  add_entry CONSTRAINED_BY LSER;
  remove_entry CONSTRAINED_BY HSER;

INTERNALS
  – internal_definitions
  OBJECTS
    NONE
  TYPES
  value IS TBD;   --| to be defined |--
  DATA
    size : constant integer := 10;
    queue : array (0. .size-1) of value;
    entries : integer := 0;   --| number of entries |--
    full : boolean := false;
    empty : boolean := true;
  CONSTANTS
    NONE
  OPERATION_SETS
    NONE
  OPERATIONS
    NONE
  EXCEPTIONS
    NONE

OBJECT_CONTROL_STRUCTURE
  -- obcs_implementation
  PSEUDO_CODE
    Declare a variable to save the parameter x.
    Loop on select for the operations:
        add_ entry : save x, end rendezvous, call OPCS
        remove_entry : call OPCS, end rendezvous
  CODE
    x_save : value;
    begin
    loop
      select
        when not full =>   --| check if queue is full |--

```
                    accept add_entry (x : IN value) do
                        x_save := x;
                    end add_entry;      --| end of rendezvous for LSER |--
                    OPCS_add_entry (x_save);
            or
                when not empty=>      --| check if queue is empty|--
                    accept remove_entry (x : OUT value) do
                        OPCS_remove_entry (x);
                    end remove_entry;      --| end of rendezvous for HSER |--
            end select;
        end loop;
```

OPERATION_CONTROL_STRUCTURES
   -- operation_definitions for terminal objects

OPERATION add_entry (x : IN value)
   DESCRIPTION
      Put value into queue and increment count. If the queue becomes full, set Boolean
      full to true.
   USED_OPERATIONS
      NONE
   PROPAGATED_EXCEPTIONS
      NONE
   HANDLED_EXCEPTIONS
      NONE
   PSEUDO_CODE
      if empty then empty := false
      put entry into queue
      entries := entries + 1
      if entries = size then full := true
   CODE
```
      if empty then
          empty := false;
      end if;
      queue (entries) := x;
      entries := entries + 1;
      if entries = size then
          full := true;
      end if;
```
END_OPERATION add_entry

OPERATION remove_entry (x : OUT value)
   DESCRIPTION
      If full, set full to false. Remove value from queue and decrement count. If the
      queue is now empty, set empty to true.
   USED_OPERATIONS
      NONE
   PROPAGATED_EXCEPTIONS
      NONE

HANDLED_EXCEPTIONS
  NONE
PSEUDO_CODE
  if full then full := false
  remove entry from queue
  entries := entries − 1
  if entries = 0 then set empty to true
CODE
  if full then
      full := false;
  end if;
  entries := entries − 1;
  x := queue (entries);
  if entries = 0 then
      empty := true;
  end if;
END_OPERATION remove_entry

END_OBJECT FIFO_Queue

2 ODS OF ACTIVE OBJECT Interrupt

OBJECT Interrupt IS ACTIVE
  PRAGMA TARGET_LANGUAGE Ada

DESCRIPTION
  This object consists of two operations to handle interrupts at addresses 101 and 101.
  Data is read from the corresponding buffer and added to a FIFO_Queue.

IMPLEMENTATION_OR_SYNCHRONISATION_CONSTRAINTS
  Each operation is attached to an interrupt, either 101 or 102. The operation shall be
  performed within 24 ms.

PROVIDED_INTERFACE
  -- provided_interface_definitions
  TYPES
    NONE
  CONSTANTS
    NONE
  OPERATION_SETS
    NONE
  OPERATIONS
    handle_101;
    handle_102;
  EXCEPTIONS
    NONE

REQUIRED_INTERFACE

-- required_interface_definitions

OBJECT FIFO_Queue;
  TYPES
    NONE
  CONSTANTS
    NONE
  OPERATION_SETS
    NONE
  OPERATIONS
    add_entry;
  EXCEPTIONS
    NONE

DATAFLOWS
    buffer => FIFO_Queue;

EXCEPTION_FLOWS
    NONE

OBJECT_CONTROL_STRUCTURE
    -- obcs_synchronisation
  DESCRIPTION
    This object has two Constrained Operations to handle the Interrupts at addresses
    101 and 102.
  CONSTRAINED_OPERATIONS
    handle_101 CONSTRAINED_BY ASER_by_IT101;
    handle_102 CONSTRAINED_BY ASER_by_IT102;

INTERNALS
    -- internal_definitions
  OBJECTS
    NONE
  TYPES
    Type t_buffer;   --| not yet defined |--
  DATA
    NONE
  CONSTANTS
    NONE
  OPERATION_SETS
    NONE
  OPERATIONS
    read_buffer (buff_no : IN integer; buffer : OUT t_buffer);
  EXCEPTIONS
    NONE

OBJECT_CONTROL_STRUCTURE
    -- obcs_implementation

  PSEUDO_CODE
    Handle two interrupts (ASER_by_IT)

```
        loop on a select
            accept handle_101
            call OPCS for handle_101
        or
            accept handle_102
            call OPCS for handle_102
        end select loop
```

CODE
```
loop
   select
        accept handle_101 do
            OPCS_handle_101;
        end handle_101;
   or
        accept handle_102 do
            OPCS_handle_102;
        end handle_102;
    end select;
end loop;
```

OPERATION_CONTROL_STRUCTURES

OPERATION handle_101
  DESCRIPTION
    Store data in FIFO_Queue.
  USED_OPERATIONS
    FIFO_Queue.add_entry;
    read_buffer;   --| internal operation |--
  PROPAGATED_EXCEPTIONS
    NONE
  HANDLED_EXCEPTIONS
    NONE
  PSEUDO_CODE
    Read data from interrupt buffer. Store data in FIFO_Queue
  CODE
    read_buffer (1, buffer);
    FIFO_Queue.add_entry (buffer);
END_OPERATION handle_101

OPERATION handle_102
  DESCRIPTION
    Store data in FIFO_Queue.
  USED_OPERATIONS
    FIFO_Queue.add_entry;
    read_buffer;   --| internal operation |--
  PROPAGATED_EXCEPTIONS
    NONE
  HANDLED_EXCEPTIONS
    NONE

PSEUDO_CODE
Read data from interrupt buffer. Store data in FIFO_Queue
CODE
read_buffer (2, buffer);
FIFO_Queue.add_entry (buffer);
END_OPERATION handle_102

OPERATION read_buffer (buff_no : IN integer;
                                    buffer : OUT t_buffer)
DESCRIPTION
Read data from interrupt buffer.
USED_OPERATIONS
NONE
PROPAGATED_EXCEPTIONS
NONE
HANDLED_EXCEPTIONS
NONE
PSEUDO_CODE
Read data from interrupt buffer.
CODE
NONE   --| address not yet defined |--
END_OPERATION read_buffer

END_OBJECT Interrupt

APPENDIX **H**

ODS OF OP_CONTROL OBJECTS start AND push

1 ODS OF OP_CONTROL OBJECT start

OBJECT start IS OP_CONTROL
　　PRAGMA TARGET_LANGUAGE Ada

DESCRIPTION
　　Op_Control Object start is used to call the corresponding operations start of
　　Objects traffic_sensors and lights to initialise them.

IMPLEMENTATION_OR_SYNCHRONISATION_CONSTRAINTS
　　NONE

PROVIDED_INTERFACE
　　NONE

REQUIRED_INTERFACE
　　-- required_interface_definitions

OBJECT traffic_sensors;
　TYPES
　　NONE
　CONSTANTS
　　NONE
　OPERATION_SETS
　　NONE
　OPERATIONS
　　start;
　EXCEPTIONS
　　NONE

OBJECT lights;
　TYPES
　　NONE

CONSTANTS
  NONE
OPERATION_SETS
  NONE
OPERATIONS
  start;
EXCEPTIONS
  NONE

DATAFLOWS
  NONE

EXCEPTION_FLOWS
  NONE

INTERNALS
  -- internal_definitions
  OBJECTS
    NONE
  TYPES
    NONE
  DATA
    NONE
  CONSTANTS
    NONE
  OPERATION_SETS
    NONE
  OPERATIONS
    NONE
  EXCEPTIONS
    NONE

OPERATION_CONTROL_STRUCTURES
  -- operation_definitions for a single operation

OPERATION start
  DESCRIPTION
    Call operations start of objects traffic_sensors and lights in turn.
  USED_OPERATIONS
    traffic_sensors.start;
    lights.start;
  PROPAGATED_EXCEPTIONS
    NONE
  HANDLED_EXCEPTIONS
    NONE
  PSEUDO_CODE
    call traffic_sensors.start
    call lights.start
  CODE
    traffic_sensors.start;

```
      lights.start;
   END_OPERATION start

END_OBJECT start
```

2 ODS OF OP_CONTROL OBJECT push

```
   OBJECT push IS OP_CONTROL
      PRAGMA TARGET_LANGUAGE Ada

   DESCRIPTION
      Op_Control Object push is used to call the corresponding operation push of Object
      active_stack.

   IMPLEMENTATION_OR_SYNCHRONISATION_CONSTRAINTS
      push may be suspended while waiting for the operation push of active_stack.

   PROVIDED_INTERFACE
      NONE

   REQUIRED_INTERFACE
      -- required_interface_definitions

   OBJECT active_stack;
      TYPES
        stack_entry
      CONSTANTS
        NONE
      OPERATION_SETS
        NONE
      OPERATIONS
        push (x : IN stack_entry);
      EXCEPTIONS
        NONE

   DATAFLOWS
      NONE

   EXCEPTION_FLOWS
      NONE

   INTERNALS
      -- internal_definitions
      OBJECTS
        NONE
      TYPES
        NONE
      DATA
        NONE
      CONSTANTS
```

NONE
OPERATION_SETS
  NONE
OPERATIONS
  NONE
EXCEPTIONS
  NONE

OPERATION_CONTROL_STRUCTURES
  -- operation_definitions for a single operation

OPERATION push (x : IN stack_entry)
  DESCRIPTION
    Call operation push of object active_stack.
  USED_OPERATIONS
    active_stack.push;
  PROPAGATED_EXCEPTIONS
    NONE
  HANDLED_EXCEPTIONS
    NONE
  PSEUDO_CODE
    call active_stack.push with stack entry.
  CODE
    active_stack.push (x);

END_OPERATION push

END OBJECT push

APPENDIX I

ADA LANGUAGE FEATURES

This appendix gives an overview of the Ada programming language to assist the reader who has no previous knowledge of Ada. A full definition of Ada according to the ANSI Standard 1815A is to be found in the *Ada Language Reference Manual*.

TYPES

A type is a pattern for a data item.

Integer type
```
type COLUMN is range 1..100;
```

Floating point type
```
type REAL is digits 5;
type Y is delta 0.125 range 0.0 .. 255.0; -- fixed point
```

Array type
```
type TABLE is array (1..10) of INTEGER;
type VECTOR is array (INTEGER range <>) of REAL;
type MATRIX is array (INTEGER range <>,INTEGER range <>) of REAL;
```

Enumeration type
```
type DAYS is (MON, TUES, WED, THURS, FRI, SAT, SUN);
```

Subtype
```
subtype WEEKDAYS is DAYS range MON .. FRI;
subtype VECTOR10 is VECTOR (1..10);
```

Derived type
```
type AN_INTEGER is new integer;
type MIDWEEK is new DAYS range TUES .. THURS;
```

Boolean type has the value FALSE or TRUE
   type HUNGRY is new BOOLEAN;

Record type
   type R is
      record
         field_1 : TABLE;
         field_2 : COLUMN;
      end record;

   type SQUARE (SIDE : INTEGER) is
      record
         MAT : MATRIX (1..SIDE, 1..SIDE);
      end record;

Access type
   type POINTER is access MATRIX;

Task type is not permitted in the Provided interface of an ODS.

DATA DECLARATIONS

   <data> : <type> [:= <value>];
   X: INTEGER := 99;
   A : MATRIX (1..2, 1..2) := ((1.0,2.0), (3.0,4.0));
   DAY : DAYS;

STATEMENTS

Assignment
   X := 1;

If statement
   if DAY = WED then
      X := 3;
   elsif DAY = FRI then
      X := 5;
   else
      X := 0;
   end if;

Case statement
   case DAY is

```
      when WED =>
          X := 3;
      when FRI =>
          X := 5;
      when others =>
          X := 0;
  end case;
```

While loop

```
  while X < 99 loop
      sum := sum + X;
      X := X + 1;
  end loop;
```

For loop

```
  for X in 1..99 loop
      factorial := factorial * X;
  end loop;
```

PACKAGES

Specification part declares visible parts of a package

```
  package SIMULATION is
      procedure START (P : INTEGER);
      procedure RUN (N : INTEGER);
      procedure REPORT;
  end SIMULATION;
```

Body part

```
  package body SIMULATION is
      procedure START (P : INTEGER) is
          LOCAL : INTEGER;      -- data declaration
      begin
          null;                     -- Ada statements here
      end START;
      procedure RUN (N : INTEGER) is separate;
      procedure REPORT is separate;
  end SIMULATION;
```

SUBPROGRAMS

Procedures

A procedure RUN (or a function) may be stored in a different file from the package body by declaring it SEPARATE as above. The procedure body is then preceded by the separate statement:

```
separate (SIMULATION)
procedure RUN (N : INTEGER) is
begin
    null;      -- code
end RUN;
```

Functions with a return type

```
function ADD (A,B : VECTOR10) return VECTOR10 is
C : VECTOR10;
begin
    for J in VECTOR10'RANGE loop
        C(J) := A(J) + B(J);
    end loop;
    return C;
end ADD;
```

A function "+" may be defined as an operator in a similar way.

TASKS

A task is the real-time feature that provides concurrent processing within Ada. A task has one or more entry points, which may be connected to a hardware address by a representation clause:

```
for ENTRY_E use at 1234;
```

Alternatively, entry points are used for intertask communication, which is called a RENDEZVOUS.

Task A will invoke task B entry point ENTRY_E in a similar way to a procedure call, i.e.:

```
B.ENTRY_E;
```

Task B will have an entry point declared in the package specification as follows:

```
task B is
    entry ENTRY_E;
end B;
```

The code to implement the entry point in the package body is:

```
accept ENTRY_E do
begin
    -- code;
end E;
```

A select statement allows multiple entry points to a task to have a selection protocol, so that a sequence may be imposed, or one of a set may be permitted entry, and an optional guard condition may be added, with a loop to allow the task to continue indefinitely:

```
        task body B is
            SECOND_TIME : BOOLEAN := FALSE;
    begin
            loop
                select
                    accept ENTRY_E do
                        SECOND_TIME := TRUE;      -- code in rendezvous
                    end ENTRY_E;
                        -- code after rendezvous here
                or
                    when SECOND_TIME =>           -- guard condition
                    accept ENTRY_F do
                        null;                     -- code in rendezvous
                    end ENTRY_F;
                end select;
            end loop;
    end B;
```

An entry may also have parameters.

EXCEPTIONS

An exception is an unusual event, which takes the program flow out of the normal path into an exception handler. An exception must be declared, and then may be *raised* in one place and *handled* in another. An exception is declared thus:

```
    MY_PROBLEM : exception;
```

One procedure may raise an exception by:

```
    raise MY_PROBLEM;
```

The procedure that called it may have as an exception handler:

```
    exception
      when MY_PROBLEM =>
        print_report;
      when others =>
        print_unknown_error;
    end PROCEDURE_NAME;
```

GENERIC PACKAGES

A generic package may have parameters of type, data or procedure which define the types of data that the package operates on, relevant data and special procedures for those types. The purpose is to allow a common function, such as queue or stack, to be implemented once and then to be reused on different entity types. A generic package for a queue may be declared as:

```
generic
    type ITEM is (<>);
package QUEUE is
    procedure PUSH (X : ITEM);
    function POP return ITEM;
end QUEUE;
```

A new package MY_QUEUE, called an instance, may be created from the generic package QUEUE thus:

```
with QUEUE;
package INSTANCE is
    type MY_TYPE is new INTEGER;      -- define a type
    package MY_QUEUE is new QUEUE (MY_TYPE);
end INSTANCE;
```

PROGRAM STRUCTURE

A program comprises a main procedure and several packages. Each package contains procedures, functions or tasks which call each other in order to make up the complete program. A package may also contain other packages.

A package may contain procedures in the package body in addition to those specified in the interface (specification part) which may be called by procedures within the package itself, but not by code in other packages.

In order to make another package visible, a context clause is used:

```
with TEXT_IO;
```

A procedure or function of TEXT_IO may then be called thus:

```
TEXT_IO.PUT_LINE ("Hello world.");
```

In order to eliminate the overhead of writing the package name each time, a Use clause may be added to give the same effect. However, this is not generally recommended in programming standards since the visibility of which package is being used is lost, making understanding and maintenance harder. Addition of the Use clause as follows:

```
use TEXT_IO;
```

allows a simple procedure call to a procedure in another package:

```
PUT_LINE ("Hello world.");
```

APPENDIX J

GLOSSARY AND ABBREVIATIONS

The figure in parenthesis refers to the section of the book in which the concept is described more fully.

Abstract data type (10.2.5) An object which encapsulates a type and its operations and operators, but without declaring a data item for the type.

Abstraction (1.2) The facility to deal with complexity by focusing on the important elements of the problem, e.g. the top level of a design, first.

Active object (4.1) An object with its own independent flow of control, in which the OBCS controls the interaction between the constrained operations of the object. An active object may be interrupt- or event-driven through a constrained operation.

Actor (4.4) An object that is not used by another object, but may use one or more other objects.

Agent (4.4) An object that is used by one or more objects, and also uses one or more other objects.

Basic Design Step (2.2) The design step that is performed on each object to provide decomposition into child objects, or to refine the object as a terminal object.

BNF of ODS (5.1) The Backus Naur Form of the Object Description Skeleton is defined in the *HOOD Reference Manual Issue 3.1.1*, Appendix C as a formal definition of the syntax of the ODS.

Child object (2.1) An object that is produced by decomposition of a parent object in the HOOD Basic Design Step.

Class object (6.1) An object template to represent a reusable object with type, constant, operation set and operation parameters.

Client (4.4) An object that uses one or more other objects, as in a client–server relationship.

Constrained operation (7.2) An operation of an active object that is constrained in its execution by the status of the object as defined in the OBCS.

Control flow (4.4) Control flow between objects is represented by the Use relationship. Control flow within an active object is represented in the OBCS.

Data flow (4.7) Flow of data in parameters of operations between used and using objects.

Encapsulation (1.2) The method of combining data and operations on those data in an object (e.g. an Ada package or C++ class).

Environment object (4.9) An object which represents the provided interface of another object used by the system to be designed, but which is not part of the HOOD design tree.

Exception flow (4.8) An abnormal return from an operation of a used object to an operation of a using object.

HOOD Chapter Skeleton (HCS) (2.4) The HCS defines the layout of the HOOD document which contains a HOOD design.

HOOD design tree (HDT) (2.1) The tree of objects of the system being designed, consisting of the root object and its successive decomposition into child objects until terminal objects are reached.

HOOD Reference Manual (HRM) The *HOOD Reference Manual* is the standard definition of the syntax and semantics of the HOOD method, issued and controlled by the HOOD User Group.

Include relationship (4.3) Expresses that a parent object is fully decomposed into a set of child objects that collectively provide the same functionality as the parent.

Information hiding (1.2) Information hiding supplements encapsulation by preventing an entity, usually data, from being visible to other software, by declaring it in the internals of an object rather than in the interface (e.g. declaration only in the body of an Ada package and not in the specification, or as a private or protected declaration in C++), or by hiding implementation details of an entity, e.g. as a private type.

Inheritance (10.3.2) The ability to define a class which is an extension of an existing class (called a base class), so that the new class *inherits* all the attributes (data and types) and all the actions (operations) of the base class.

Instance object (6.3) An object that is created for a design from a class object.

Internal operation (5.7) An operation that is defined in a terminal object to support the implementation of Provided operations.

Multiple inheritance (10.3.2) The potential for a class to inherit from more than one base class.

Non-terminal object (2.1) An object which is decomposed into child objects (parent object).

Object (3.1) An encapsulation of data or a hardware interface with the operations to access and change it, with relevant type definitions, constants and exceptions.

Object Control Structure (OBCS) (5) Part of the ODS that defines the control flow between constrained operations.

Object Description Skeleton (ODS) (5) The formal notation of the design of an object.

Object-oriented (10.3.2) The essence of an object-oriented method is the identification and development of a design using an object as the basic building block of the design. The term 'object-oriented' is often taken to imply development of classes as well as objects, so that the executable design consists of objects as instances of these classes.

Op_Control object (7) An object that implements the mapping between one parent operation and multiple operations of child objects.

Operation (3.3) An action that is performed on an object, to be represented by a procedure or function in Ada.

Operation Control Structure (OPCS) (5) Part of the ODS that defines the logic of the operation (external or internal) in terms of pseudocode.

Operation_set (4.6) A shorthand form for a set of operations which precludes the necessity to write long lists of operations in a HOOD diagram.

Overloading (10.3.2) The ability for an operation name to be repeated within the definition of a single object, providing that there is some way of differentiating between them, i.e. by having different parameter and result type profiles in Ada, or different argument signature in C++.

Parent object (2.1) An object that is decomposed into child objects.

Passive object (4.1) An object which provides only unconstrained operations, and which does not have its own independent control flow but executes in the control flow of the client object that uses it.

Polymorphism (10.3.2) The ability for the selection of an operation body to be determined at run time, according to the class of the object to which the operation is currently referring.

Pragma (5.10, 7.3.3) A HOOD pragma is a command to a HOOD tool to specify a criterion for Ada code generation.

Provided interface (5.3) Part of the ODS that defines the interface of the object.

Pseudocode (5.9) A means of defining the logic in structured natural language (e.g. English) as detailed design prior to coding in the target language. Pseudocode is used in the OBCS and the OPCS.

Required interface (5.4) Part of the ODS that defines the interfaces of used objects.

Root object (2.3.1) The top-level object which represents the system to be designed.

Server (4.4) An object that does not use another object, but provides services and is used by one or more other objects.

Standard Interchange Format (10.4) The Standard Interchange Format (SIF) is defined in the *HOOD Reference Manual Issue 3.1.1*, Appendix E, as a standard ASCII text format for the export and import of a HOOD design, to be used for transfer of designs between HOOD tools from different vendors or between different hardware platforms.

Terminal object (2.3.2) An object at the bottom of the HOOD design tree which is not decomposed into child objects.

Uncle object (4.5) An object that is used by a parent object appears as an uncle object in the diagram of that parent, and is used by at least one child of the parent object.

Unconstrained operation (4.2) An operation which responds immediately to a call from another object, and executes in the flow of control of the using object.

Use relationship (4.4) An object is said to use another object if the using object requires one or more of the operations provided by the used object.

Virtual node object (VN) (9.1) An object which is used to partition the HOOD design tree for distribution across two or more processors.

AD	architectural design
ADD	Architectural Design Document
AM	abstract machine
ANNA	Annotated Ada
ANSI	American National Standards Institute
ASCII	American Standard Code for Interchange of Information
ASER	asynchronous execution request
BNF	Backus Naur Form
CNES	Centre Nationale des Etudes Spatiaux
COLOS	Columbus Operating System
CORE	Controlled Requirement Expression
DD	detailed design
DDD	Detailed Design Document
DFD	data flow diagram
DPT	design process tree
EFA	European Fighter Aircraft
ERD	entity relation diagram
ESA	European Space Agency
Estec	European Space Technology Centre
FIFO	first in first out
HCS	HOOD Chapter Skeleton
HDT	HOOD design tree
HOOD	hierarchical object-oriented design
HRM	*HOOD Reference Manual*
HSER	highly synchronous execution request
HTG	HOOD Technical Group
HUG	HOOD User Group
HUM	*HOOD User Manual*
JSD	Jackson Structured Design
LSER	loosely synchronous execution request
LTR	langage temps réele
OBCS	Object Control Structure
ODS	Object Description Skeleton
OOA	object-oriented analysis
OOD	object-oriented design
OOP	object-oriented programming
OPCS	Operation Control Structure
PDL	Program Design Language
SA/SD	structured analysis/structured design
SADT	Structured Analysis and Design Technique
SIF	Standard Interchange Format
SRD	Software Requirements Document
STD	state transition diagram
STD	system to design
TOER	timed out execution request
VN	virtual node (object)
VNT	virtual node tree

BIBLIOGRAPHY

The following is a useful list of books and papers on HOOD, Ada and OOD. Those referenced in the text are indicated by an asterisk.

Ada Language Reference Manual, ANSI/MIL-STD 1815A.

*Atkinson, Colin, Trevor Moreton and Antonio Natali, *Ada for Distributed Systems*, Ada Companion Series (Cambridge University Press, 1988). This book introduces a virtual node concept in chapter 3.

*Booch, Grady, *Software Engineering with Ada*, Ada Companion Series (Benjamin Cummings, 1983).

Booch, Grady, Object-oriented development, *IEEE Transactions on Software Engineering*, Vol. SE-12, Feb. 1986.

Booch, Grady, *Object-Oriented Design with Applications* (Benjamin Cummings, 1991).

*Booch, Grady, *Software Components in Ada* (Benjamin Cummings, 1987).

*Board for Software Standardisation and Control (BSSC), *ESA Software Engineering Standards*, PSS–05–5, Issue 1, Jan. 1987.

Buhr, Raymond J.A., *System Design with Ada* (Prentice Hall, 1985).

*Coad, Peter and Edward Yourdon, *Object-Oriented Analysis*, 2nd edn (Yourdon Press Computing Series, 1991).

Coad, Peter and Edward Yourdon, *Object Oriented Design* (Yourdon Press Computing Series, 1991).

Galinier, Michel and A. Mathis, *Guide du Concepteur MACH* (Thomson CSF, DSE and IGL Technology, 1985).

*HOOD User Group, *HOOD Reference Manual Issue 3.1.1* (Masson/Prentice Hall International, 1992).

*HOOD Working Group, *HOOD User Manual Issue 3.0* (European Space Agency, 1989, WME/89–353/JB).

Labreuille, Bertrand and Maurice Heitz, Hierarchical object-oriented design and Ada, *Proceedings of the Ada-Europe Conference, Munich*, Ada Companion Series (Cambridge University Press, 1987).

Lynch, Barry (ed.), Ada: experiences and prospects, *Proceedings of the Ada-Europe Conference Dublin*, Ada Companion Series (Cambridge University Press, 1990). The following papers are recommended:

di Giovanni, Raffaele, On the translation of HOOD nets into Ada.

Chandler, Simon, Reducing the risk of using Ada on-board the Columbus Manned Space Elements.

Lai, Michel, Why not combine HOOD and Ada? An overview of several French Navy projects.

*Meyer, Bertrand, *Object-oriented Software Construction* (Prentice Hall International, 1988).

Parnas, David L., Designing software for ease of extension and contraction, *IEEE Transactions on Software Engineering*, Vol. SE-5, No. 2, 1979.

Robinson, Peter (ed.), *Object-oriented Design* (Chapman and Hall, 1992).

Seidewitz and Stark, *General Object Oriented Software Development*, NASA Software Engineering Laboratory Series SEL-86-002.

Shlaer, Sally and Stephen J. Mellor, *Object-Oriented Systems Analysis* (Yourdon Press, 1988).

Shlaer, Sally and Stephen J. Mellor, *Object-Orientated Lifecycles* (Prentice Hall International, 1991).

Wellings, Andrew, Distributed execution – units of partitioning, *Proceedings of the International Workshop on Ada Real Time Issues*, *ACM ADA LETTERS*, Vol. 7, Fall 1988.

*Wellings, Andrew and Alan Burns, Hard real-time HOOD: a design method for hard real-time Ada9X systems, *Towards Ada 9X: Proceedings of the 1991 Ada UK International Conference* (IOS Press, 1991).

INDEX

abstract data type, 33, 162, 227
abstract machines, 6
abstraction, 7, 100, 227
acceptance, 1, 2
active design, 55
active object, 52, 82, 85, 114, 143, 227
actor, 227
actor–agent–server, 60
Ada, 1, 5, 6
Ada design method, 1
Ada pragma PRIORITY, 97
Ada language:
   data, 222
   exception, 225
   function, 224
   generic package, 225
   package, 223
   procedure, 223
   program structure, 226
   task, 54, 114, 117, 224
   task type, 173
   type, 221
Ada source code, 86, 93, 120, 156, 169
agent, 227
ANNA (ANNotated Ada), 6
application domain approach, 9
applicaton domain library, 10
architectural design, 1, 4, 67, 86, 94, 113, 163, 166
Architectural Design Document, 4, 23
architectural design method, 1
ASER for interrupt, 117
asynchronous, 54, 145
asynchronous execution request (ASER), 86,
   116, 121
asynchronous model, 112
attribute, 29
Auto-G, 6

Bank Account, 29
Basic Design Step, 11, 14, 19, 20, 21, 101, 104,
   149, 156, 175, 227
BNF of ODS, 227
Booch, Grady, 6, 26, 41, 232

C++, 171
C++ class, 33
candidate objects, 35
candidate operations, 38
CASE tool, 22, 23, 155
child object, 11, 56, 88, 227
CISI Ingenierie, 2, 3
class, 9, 26
class object, 32, 83, 100, 101, 164, 204, 227
client, 227
code review, 166
coding, 4
cohesion, 8
Columbus Space Station, 3, 5, 6, 25, 143, 156
communication protocol, 145
completeness, 169
computer aided software engineering (CASE), 2
concurrency, 114
configurability, 9
configuration control, 173
configuration management, 5
constant, 81, 83, 89
constrained operation, 48, 54, 56, 86, 115, 119,
   227
constraints, 79
context diagram, 14, 48
control flow, 52, 59, 228
control flow diagrams, 4
Coral, 5
CORE, 26, 43, 169, 170
CRI A/S, 2, 3

Cross-reference Reports, 168
cyclic use, 64

data, 88, 91
data entities, 8
data flow, 4, 67, 84, 228
data flow diagram, 6, 14, 25
data flow diagram approach, 43
dataflow, 81
decomposition, 56
decomposition hierarchy, 30
definition of an object, 33
design, 5
design process, 11
design review, 166
detailed design, 4, 6, 94, 166
Detailed Design Document, 4, 23
development of solution strategy, 16
distributed program, 148
distribution, 143
documentation, 8

Eiffel, 171
embedded software, 2
embedded system, 1, 11
encapsulate, 144
encapsulation, 8, 28, 100, 228
entity relation attribute, 29
entity relation diagrams, 26
environment object, 72, 102, 160, 228
equipment requirements, 4
ESA software engineering life-cycle, 3
ESA software engineering standards PSS-05-0, 3
Estec, 2
European Fighter Aircraft, 3
European Space Agency, 1
exception, 82, 83, 90, 93
exception flow, 69, 84, 228
extensibility, 9

FIFO_Queue example, 210
finding objects, 25
formal parameters, 83, 102, 103, 106
formalisation of the solution, 18
formalisation of the strategy, 17
French Space Agency CNES, 5
function, 92

graphical description, 17
Guerin, Michel, 2

hardware interface, 28
hardware interrupt, 117
heating system, 48, 56, 180
Hermes Spaceplane, 3
highly synchronous, 54
highly synchronous execution request (HSER),
    86, 115, 120

HOOD Chapter Skeleton, 22, 165, 177, 228
HOOD design, 72
HOOD design process, 28
HOOD design tree, 11, 23, 56, 101, 160, 173,
    228
HOOD diagram, 105
HOOD diagrams, 51
HOOD document, 23
HOOD documentation, 156
HOOD object, 27
HOOD pragma, 97
HOOD pragma HCS, 173
HOOD Reference Manual, 3, 23, 228
HOOD rules, 3, 62, 65, 156, 164, 167
HOOD text approach, 34
HOOD toolset, 2, 4, 173
HOOD User Group, 3, 155
HOOD User Manual, 3, 5
HOOD Working Group, 3
HSER, 120

Implemented_By link, 57, 88, 110
Include relationship, 56, 228
information hiding, 7, 228
inheritance, 100, 110, 171, 228
inspection, 165
instance object, 102, 104, 207, 228
instance parameters, 104
integrated programming support environment,
    5
integration test, 4
integration test review, 166
interface, 4, 29, 51
    checks, 167
    control, 30
internal operation, 228
Internals, 87
interrupt, 47, 112, 114, 117, 123, 213
    address, 86

Jackson Structured Design, 6
justification of design decisions, 18, 168

label, 86, 115
locality, 8
loosely synchronous, 54, 145
loosely synchronous execution request (LSER),
    86, 116, 121

maintainability, 8
mapping, 8
Mascot-3, 6
Matra Espace, 2, 3
Meyer, Bertrand, 27, 41, 233
mode, 92
models of use, 64
modularity, 8
multiple inheritance, 228

NASA, 1

object, 9, 17, 228
Object Control Structure (OBCS), 53, 78, 85,
    114, 119, 147, 228
object definiton, 25, 78
Object Descripton Skeleton (ODS), 19, 75, 102,
    106, 128, 148, 173, 228
ODS BNF, 174
object identification, 17
object life-cycle, 5, 169
object operation table, 17, 39, 55
object-oriented, 229
object-oriented analysis, 28, 40, 171, 232
object-oriented design, 6, 101
object-oriented programming, 171
Object_type, 79
Op_Control object, 89, 126, 217, 229
operation, 41, 55, 81, 83, 89, 229
Operation Control Structure (OPCS), 43, 78,
    91, 229
operation declaration, 92
operation identification, 17
operation_set, 66, 81, 83, 89, 229
operations, 41, 55, 81
overloading, 42, 172, 229

package body, 88
package specification, 162
parameter name, 92
parent object, 11, 56, 88, 229
passive design, 54
passive object, 114, 51, 229
Pearl, 5
petri nets, 6, 26
polymorphism, 100, 172, 229
pragma, 229
    ALLOCATED_TO, 98
    EXCEPTION, 98
    FIFO, 125
    GROUP, 125
    HCS, 97
    MAIN, 98
    SERVER_TASK, 125
    TARGET_LANGUAGE, 97
prime contractor, 4
problem definition, 15
problem domain, 40
procedure, 92
process-oriented, 6
productivity, 9
Program Design Language (PDL), 2, 5, 6, 75
project approach, 101
prototyping, 163
Provided interface, 55, 73, 79, 229
pseudocode, 4, 6, 86, 93, 94, 120, 229

quality, 101

quality assurance, 2, 3, 4, 22, 42, 157, 166,
    167

real-time software, 112
real-world entity, 8
remote rendezvous, 143
Required interface, 82, 104, 229
Required operation, 93
requirement references, 5
requirement trace, 168
requirement verification, 165
requirements, 4, 5
reserved words, 178
reusability, 8
reuse, 100, 160
review, 166
root object, 11, 20, 55, 229

SADT, 5, 6, 170
seniority hierarchy, 30, 60
server, 229
set of processors, 143
shared memory, 144
Software Development Environment, 5, 156,
    173
software development life-cycle, 159
software engineering life-cycle, 1, 22, 75
software engineering standards, 7
software interrupt, 117
software layers, 9
Software Requirements Document, 4, 25
software sciences, 3
solution domain, 41
solution strategy, 35
    development of, 16
Spacelab, 1
specification, 30
specification part, 79
Standard Interchange Format, 23, 173, 229
standards, 22, 169
state, 41
    of an object, 26
state machine, 33
state transition diagram, 26, 33, 159
structured analysis, 6
structured design, 6
subsystem requirements, 4
synchronous model, 112
system configuration, 102, 160
system requirements, 4

Technical Research Program, 2
terminal object, 12, 21, 88, 91, 229
testing, 4, 164
timed out execution request (TOER), 86, 117,
    121
timeout, 54
timing budget, 53

traffic lights system, 36, 45, 181
training course, 2
trigger arrow, 86, 115
type package, 161
types, 80, 83, 88

uncle object, 12, 65, 229
unconstrained operation, 81, 230
Use relationship, 59, 230
used operations, 93

User Requirements Document, 4

validation, 4, 164, 166
verification, 4, 164, 165
virtual machine, 9
virtual node object (VN), 143, 230

walkthrough, 165

Yourdon, 6, 26, 170